# THIRTY TIME-TESTED TIPS FOR
# FRESHWATER FISHING

**from the Editors of
In-Fisherman Magazine**

Published by
In-Fisherman®

## In-Fisherman
A PRIMEDIA Company

# The In-Fisherman Secrets Series

## THIRTY MORE TIME-TESTED TIPS FOR
# FRESHWATER FISHING

Publisher *Stuart Legaard*

Editor In Chief *Doug Stange*

Editors *Dave Csanda, Steve Hoffman,*
*Steve Quinn, Matt Straw*

Staff Writer *Jeff Simpson*

Project Coordinator *Scott Lawrence*

Copy Editor *Joann Phipps with J. Z. Grover*

Primary Writer *Steve Hoffman*

Layout & Design *Jim Pfaff with Scott Lawrence*

ISBN 1-892947-03-X
**The In-Fisherman Secrets Series**
An
$F$ (Fish) + $L$ (Location) + $P$ (Presentation) = $S$ (Success)™
Educational Service

First Edition, 1999

# TABLE OF CONTENTS

# INTRODUCTION

**S**ome anglers always seem to catch fish. These anglers are always a new technique or two or a new bait or two ahead of the rest. When the hordes toss spinners and spoons, this bunch works plastics. When everyone else fishes during the day, they fish at night. When the fishing pressure is on weedbeds, they move to rocks, or look deeper, or move to open water. And when they can't move, can't escape the crowd, they use finesse techniques where standard techniques are the norm; or they modify a standard technique when finesse is the norm. A new bait, a new technique, an old standard modified. A fake here, a sleight of hand there. Understanding when to zig instead of zag is part of the process, part of what In-Fisherman is about.

Fishing is a break, a chance to get away from it all and escape the hustle and bustle of the workaday world. But most anglers also want to catch fish, and it is this part of the process that In-Fisherman has addressed for more than 25 years.

We are about teaching anglers how to catch more fish. The thrill of fishing is in the pursuit, the challenge of getting to know the characteristics of each fish species, in order to make judgments about where to find them and how to catch them.

*Thirty Time-Tested Tips For Freshwater Fishing* is gleaned from thousands of in-depth articles featured over the years in *In-Fisherman* magazine.

***How to use this book***—Each tip follows a format that includes a short introduction, capturing the essence of the event, followed by tackle recommendations to help you fish efficiently. Seasonal icons suggest the seasons during which a tip applies—spring 🌱 , summer ☀ , fall 🍂 , winter ❄ . And finally, a technical section addresses details about location (finding fish) and presentation (getting them to bite). Illustrations that accompany each tip result from thousands of hours of pleasant research.

Welcome to a small part of the world of In-Fisherman. For more about fishing, contact us at In-Fisherman, Two In-Fisherman Dr., Brainerd, MN 56425. Or visit us on the Internet at <www.in-fisherman.com>.

*Doug Stange*
*Editor In Chief*

# CAROLINA RIGGING FOR LARGEMOUTHS

A s with most fishing techniques, popularity spawns innovation. In many ways, Carolina rigs parallel livebait rigs for walleyes—sliding sinkers, swivels, beads, and leaders. But while walleye anglers often adjust sinker weight and color, add beads, and adjust leader length, most bass fishermen tie on a 3/4-ounce weight, a single red bead, and a 24- to 30-inch leader.

## When

## Leaders

Match your leader length to the season or type of cover you're fishing. Short, 1½- to 3-foot leaders work well during spring and winter when bass hold tight to the structure and you need a precise presentation. But for bass holding along steep ledges or suspended outside a break, as often happens in summer and fall, a longer leader shines. Leaders up to 7 feet long allow baits to drift slowly, giving bass a longer look at the bait.

## Flotation

Check the flotation of your plastic baits. Most sink slowly on a standard 4/0 hook, though some may float a small hook or achieve neutral buoyancy with a large hook. To float baits higher above weed clumps, stumps, or other cover, try a floating jighead, styrofoam floats, or thicker diameter leader material.

# Sinkers

Brass weights have gained enormous popularity with Carolina rig enthusiasts in recent years. Brass is less dense than lead, but clicks more sharply against rocks and beads. To maximize the clicking sounds that may help attract bass in deep clear water and shallow murky water, some anglers add a brass collar between the sinker and the bead. To minimize the flash that may spook bass, some manufacturers have dyed their brass weights black.

# Rattles

Rattling lures sometimes catch more bass than non-rattling versions. Plastic and glass rattle chambers filled with shot slide into soft plastic baits. Rattles are activated when the bait hits bottom or when it's shaken. Snap-on rattles of similar design can be attached to or removed from a hook shank in seconds. Some manufacturers also offer brass weights with shot inside to produce both rattling and clicking sounds. ☐

## *Carolina Options*

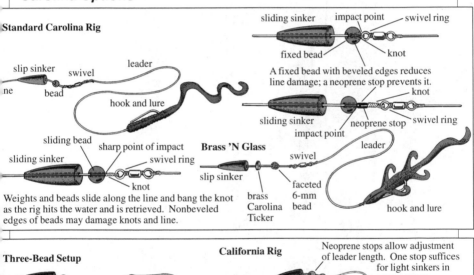

**Standard Carolina Rig**

sliding sinker    impact point    swivel ring
fixed bead    knot

A fixed bead with beveled edges reduces line damage; a neoprene stop prevents it.

knot
sliding sinker    neoprene stop    swivel ring
impact point

slip sinker    swivel    leader
ne    bead
hook and lure

**Brass 'N Glass**    leader
swivel
slip sinker
faceted
brass    6-mm
Carolina    bead
Ticker
hook and lure

sliding bead    sharp point of impact
sliding sinker    swivel ring
knot

Weights and beads slide along the line and bang the knot as the rig hits the water and is retrieved. Nonbeveled edges of beads may damage knots and line.

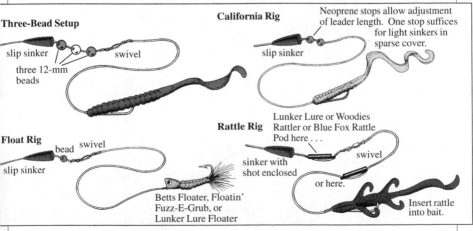

**Three-Bead Setup**

slip sinker    swivel
three 12-mm
beads

**California Rig**    Neoprene stops allow adjustment of leader length. One stop suffices for light sinkers in sparse cover.

slip sinker

**Rattle Rig**    Lunker Lure or Woodies Rattler or Blue Fox Rattle Pod here . . .

**Float Rig**    swivel
bead
slip sinker

swivel
sinker with
shot enclosed

or here.

Insert rattle into bait.

Betts Floater, Floatin' Fuzz-E-Grub, or Lunker Lure Floater

# TWINSPINS FOR LARGEMOUTHS

The Twinspin. Forgotten bass lure. The precursor to the modern spinnerbait and forerunner of today's rubber-legged jig. The twinspin has always been ahead of its time. Today, it contends to be a potent hybrid of those two standard designs, a lure particularly good for bass in cold water. Most of the tackle industry (and most anglers) assume that in-line spinners and modern spinner-baits have made twinspins obsolete. But veteran bass fish-ermen across North America depend on twinspins of varying designs to produce bass when other baits fail.

**When**

## Tackle

*Rod:* 6- to 7-foot medium-heavy casting rod. *Reel:* large-capacity baitcasting reel. *Line:* 12- to 17-pound-test mono.

## Rigging

One-half- to three-quarter-ounce baits are effective for scratching bluff walls in deep reservoirs, while 3/8-ounce models are good for working mid-depth flats in lakes. In either situation, pork frogs and eels add to the twinspin's undulating and buoyant appearance. The result is the kind of bulky package that big bass engulf, though the strike often is detectable only as extra weight on the line.

# Presentation

During fall, twinspins are tough to beat. When water temperatures begin to drop and the cabbage starts to thin, bass often form tight groups among clumps of coontail growing in about 8 to 14 feet of water. Swim a twinspin through the clumps and you'll often catch the biggest bass in the group. Twinspins are most effective when water temperatures fall into the low 50°F range, and they remain effective into the low 40°F range.

In reservoirs across the Mid-South and California, during winter, trophy bass specialists use twinspins to catch lethargic bass holding tight to vertical bluff walls or to the bottom. When fishing steep ledges, hold the boat over deep water and cast toward the bank. Let the lure free fall near the wall, repeating the drop on each ledge until the lure falls deeper than bass are holding. For fish on the bottom, use an ultraslow retrieve. Let the bait rest on the bottom for several seconds before pumping it slowly forward. □

## Basic Presentation

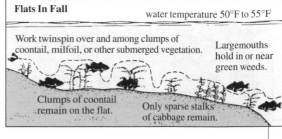

**Flats In Fall**   water temperature 50°F to 55°F

Work twinspin over and among clumps of coontail, milfoil, or other submerged vegetation.

Largemouths hold in or near green weeds.

Clumps of coontail remain on the flat.

Only sparse stalks of cabbage remain.

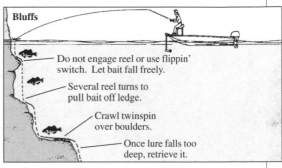

**Bluffs**

Do not engage reel or use flippin' switch. Let bait fall freely.

Several reel turns to pull bait off ledge.

Crawl twinspin over boulders.

Once lure falls too deep, retrieve it.

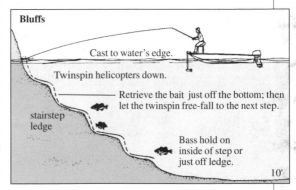

**Bluffs**

Cast to water's edge.

Twinspin helicopters down.

Retrieve the bait just off the bottom; then let the twinspin free-fall to the next step.

stairstep ledge

Bass hold on inside of step or just off ledge.

10'

## Modern Twinspin Designs

# DOCK STRATEGIES FOR LARGEMOUTH BASS

**D**ocks, boathouses, and piers become more important cover for large-mouth bass as homes are built on lakes, reservoirs, and rivers. Shoreline development often means loss of natural cover like fallen trees, stumps, lily pad beds, and submerged weeds. Shallow-loving largemouths find steel, styrofoam, and pine board a suitable substitute. But like other popular patterns, success depends on timely tactics, attention to detail, and appropriate tackle.

## When

Water temperatures above 40°F.

## Tackle

*Tubes and prerigged worms:* 6- to 7-foot medium-power spinning rod, medium-size spinning reel, and 8- to 12-pound-test mono. *Worms and soft jerkbaits:* 6½- to 7-foot medium-power spinning rod, large capacity spinning reel, and 17- to 20-pound-test mono. *Jigs:* 5½- to 6-foot medium-power pistol-grip casting rod, baitcasting reel with adjustable spool brakes, and 17- to 20-pound-test mono.

### *Anatomy Of A Productive Dock*

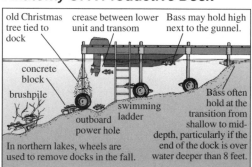

old Christmas tree tied to dock

crease between lower unit and transom

Bass may hold high next to the gunnel.

concrete block

brushpile

outboard power hole

swimming ladder

Bass often hold at the transition from shallow to mid-depth, particularly if the end of the dock is over water deeper than 8 feet.

In northern lakes, wheels are used to remove docks in the fall.

# Presentation

In murky water, crankbaits or spinnerbaits retrieved parallel to dock posts or walkways often draw strikes. Twitching a minnowbait or popping a topwater works fine too, on calm days when bass roam the front edges of docks. Most of the time, however, bass hold back under docks where traditional casting techniques can't reach. Skip tube baits and plastic worms under docks with a sidearm cast, and trigger neutral bass with a slow, steady retrieve. Soft plastic jerkbaits, weighted or unweighted, can also be cast far back under docks for inactive largemouths. Let the bait settle to the bottom, give it a slight twitch, and repeat. Set the hook when you feel any resistance. Zipping 3/16- to 3/8-ounce jigs under docks takes more practice, but often pulls fish out of brush piles and weeds that other lures can't penetrate. □

## Choosing Docks

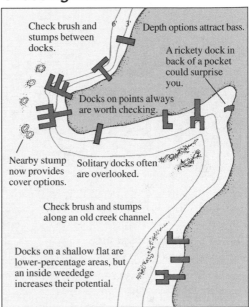

Check brush and stumps between docks.

Depth options attract bass.

A rickety dock in back of a pocket could surprise you.

Docks on points always are worth checking.

Nearby stump now provides cover options.

Solitary docks often are overlooked.

Check brush and stumps along an old creek channel.

Docks on a shallow flat are lower-percentage areas, but an inside weededge increases their potential.

## Lures For Docks

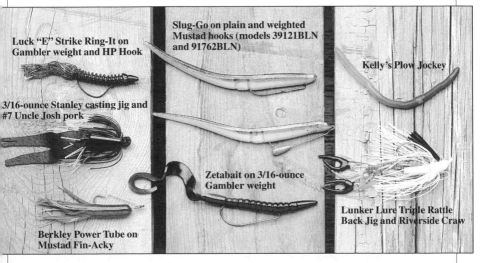

Luck "E" Strike Ring-It on Gambler weight and HP Hook

Slug-Go on plain and weighted Mustad hooks (models 39121BLN and 91762BLN)

Kelly's Plow Jockey

3/16-ounce Stanley casting jig and #7 Uncle Josh pork

Zetabait on 3/16-ounce Gambler weight

Lunker Lure Triple Rattle Back Jig and Riverside Craw

Berkley Power Tube on Mustad Fin-Acky

# SMALL BAITS FOR BIG LARGEMOUTHS IN PONDS

Small waters often call for small baits. Farm ponds covering but a few acres often hold the biggest bass in the country. While these bass may put on weight by eating quarter-pound bluegills, they often shy from big baits in all but the least-fished waters. Pond bass seem particularly familiar with their surroundings and most suspicious of intrusions.

## When

## Tackle

*Rod:* 6- to 7-foot light- or medium-light-power spinning rod. *Reel:* medium-capacity spinning reel. *Line:* 4- to 8-pound-test limp monofilament.

## Rigging

Tiny tubes, worms from 4 to 6 inches long, or miniature minnows like Normark's 1/8-ounce Rapala or Fenwick's 2-inch Pins Minnow score best when waters first warm in spring. Later, little crankbaits and spinnerbaits that run horizontally score best as ponds stratify, lowering oxygen levels in bottom waters.

In-line spinners like Mepps numerous models or the Blue Fox Vibrax offer a change of pace from late spring through fall. Their high-frequency vibrations, achieved at slow retrieve speeds, often trigger fish that will hit nothing else. At dusk, when pond bass sip wayward grasshoppers, topwaters like Arbogast's miniature Hula Popper or Jitterbug, or small prop plugs sometimes prove irresistible.

Fall calls for further downsizing with compact light jigs backed with Uncle Josh #101 pork chunks or teeny craws, plus crappie-style grubs. On pleasant days that spur more fish activity in fall, slow rolling small blades through brush shelters or bobbing crankbaits over flats works well.

# Location

Mini-baits are most effective in shallow water because the baits land softly and move quietly and naturally through the aquatic environment. Also, most small lures won't run deep enough to reach bass holding deeper than about five feet. Mini-jigs and worms also fall slowly and perform best in shallow areas. One exception is in clear ponds where small plastics often work well deep. ☐

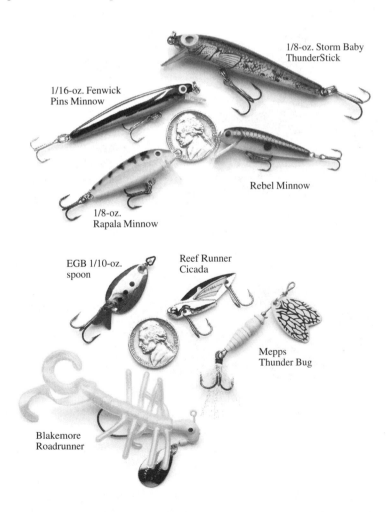

1/8-oz. Storm Baby ThunderStick

1/16-oz. Fenwick Pins Minnow

Rebel Minnow

1/8-oz. Rapala Minnow

EGB 1/10-oz. spoon

Reef Runner Cicada

Mepps Thunder Bug

Blakemore Roadrunner

# POPPERS AND CHUGGERS FOR LARGEMOUTHS

**P**oppers, chuggers, spitters. Call 'em as you see 'em. They've emerged as the hottest topwater baits of our time. And oh the fun of them. Only a tournament angler wouldn't prefer to catch a 5-pounder on a topwater lure over a 7-pounder on a crankbait. And while poppers and chuggers are in their prime during summer, they'll also catch bass shortly after ice-out and continue to produce through late fall when bass hold near shallow wood and remaining clumps of vegetation.

## When

## Tackle

*Rod:* 5½- to 6½-foot medium-power casting rod. *Reel:* medium-capacity bait-casting reel. *Line:* 6- to 10-pound abrasion-resistant monofilament for lighter baits and 12- to 17-pound line for heavier versions.

# Presentation

There's no wrong way to fish a popper, but sometimes some actions are better than others.

*Slow Retrieves:* For bass in thick weedbeds or under wood cover, the splash down and sharp bloops and long pauses of a slowly retrieved bait alerts them that something's there. The surface commotion suggests a small fish in its death throes, or maybe a frog hopping off a lily pad. Splashes, too, can stimulate bass to feed, as they think another fish has snatched a prey from the surface.

These cues may cause bass to approach cautiously or sometimes to zoom in on a lure for a closer look. A subtle twitch may provide the final trigger for a strike. Or the skirted tail quivering in current can motivate an aggressive strike. At night, slow intermittent retrieves give bass the opportunity to approach the lure, then strike. They may hit but miss fast-moving baits, especially if they move erratically.

*Fast Retrieves:* Another key retrieve for poppers is the spittin' skittering action that's become standard for summertime fishing on shad-filled reservoirs. Many modern poppers are designed more for spitting than popping. The mouth is moderate size, and the lower lip is considerable shorter than the upper lip. Its leading edges are sharp.

But versatile topwater anglers should view retrieves as a continuum of speeds and actions between the extremes of a fast spit and a bloop-and-die cadence. On a given day, a special surface dance can make the difference in the bait's attraction. While a few time-tested retrieves that need no concentration to execute are good to have, breaking the mold can sometimes pay off. □

## *Popular Poppers*

Rebel Pop-R

Yo-Zuri Pop-N-Splash

Buddha Baits Pop-Fire

Mann's Chug-N-Spit

Arbogast Hula Popper

Excalibur Pop'n Image

Rapala Skitter Pop

Storm Rattlin' Chug Bug

# SUSPENDING BAITS FOR SMALLMOUTH

For years, trophy small-mouth specialists have been crafting neutrally buoyant minnowbaits by winding pieces of wire solder around a treble hook—adding or removing metal until the bait barely floats in a tub of water. Properly weighted, these modified jerkbaits suspend and hover almost motionless when the retrieve is stopped. A presumptive preyfish hovering in front of a bass tempts even the most lethargic fish. And the longer the bait remains in front of the fish, the better your chances of getting a strike. This presentation is particularly effective for big bass in clear lakes and reservoirs.

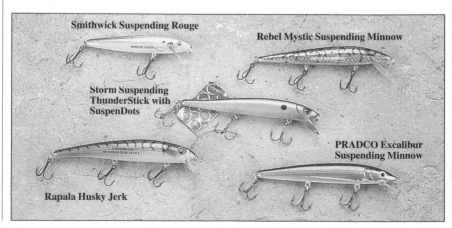

Smithwick Suspending Rouge

Rebel Mystic Suspending Minnow

Storm Suspending ThunderStick with SuspenDots

PRADCO Excalibur Suspending Minnow

Rapala Husky Jerk

# When

## Tackle

*Rod:* 5½- to 6-foot light- to medium-light-power fast-action spinning rod.
*Reel:* medium-capacity spinning reel. *Line:* 8- to 12-pound-test mono.

## Rigging

All suspending baits are built to suspend at a certain water temperature. If a suspending bait floats in say 70°F or 80°F water, it will suspend in cooler temperatures—the increased water density holds the bait down. Storm SuspenDots and SuspenStrips are adhesive dots and strips of lead that can be attached to a lure to fine-tune buoyancy. Placing SuspenDots near the lure's balance point allows the bait to suspend horizontally, while Dots placed near the lip cause the lure to hang nose down and dive up to 10 percent deeper.

## Presentation

When water temperatures fall below 50°F, it's important to work baits slowly for inactive smallmouths. Make a short sweep with your rod tip and let the lure hang motionless for 10 or 15 seconds. As water temperatures warm into the mid-50°F range, work the bait faster with longer sweeps. Jerk the bait a couple times and let it glide to a stop. Work parallel to cover, drop-offs, or weedlines, to keep the lure in the strike zone for the longest possible time. In warmer water, retrieve a nose-weighted bait quickly over shallow rock or wood cover. When the lure strikes an object, let it hang motionless for several seconds to trigger curious fish. □

1- to 2-foot sweep

### *Minnowbait Sweep*

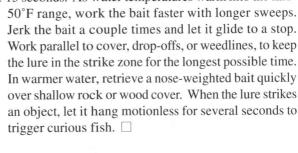

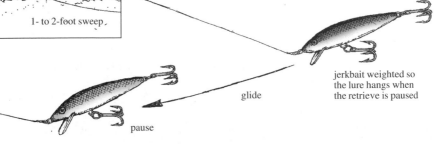

jerkbait weighted so the lure hangs when the retrieve is paused

glide

pause

# PRIME TIME CRANKIN' FOR SMALLMOUTHS

No magic temperature in fishing? Apparently, smallmouths don't know that. Top smallmouth anglers around the country point to 48°F as a key water temperature in spring. Fish are in the same areas they've been using for weeks, but suddenly they're more likely to be aggressive. Party time. Smallmouth Mardi Gras. And for the first time since fall, smallies are chasing crankbaits.

## When

Water temperatures
between 42°F and 55°F.

## Tackle

*Rod:* 7-foot fast-action medium-power spinning rod. *Reel:* medium-capacity spinning reel. *Line:* 8- to 10-pound-test mono.

## Presentation

In natural lakes and mid-depth reservoirs, smallmouths move toward hard-bottom spawning flats at the end of the Coldwater Period. Shoreline lips, rock edges, and drop-offs attract and hold the largest concentrations of active fish. Particularly in natural lakes, smallmouths may also hold near docks. Early on, key docks are close to deep water. Later, almost any dock on a hard-bottom spawning flat becomes a potential draw.

Water temperature is a guideline for locating fish and determining their activity level. At the end of the Coldwater Period, a slow and steady retrieve triggers smallmouths that won't pursue a fast moving lure. Cast out and give the reel handle a few quick turns to get the bait down to the proper depth. Retrieve at the slowest speed that will maintain that depth.

As water temperature approaches 48°F, smallmouths become increasingly active and move into shallower water.

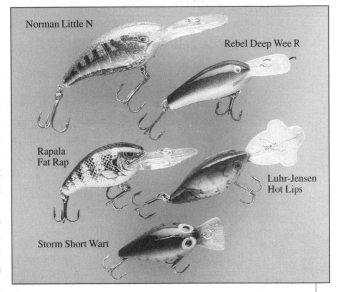

Norman Little N

Rebel Deep Wee R

Rapala Fat Rap

Luhr-Jensen Hot Lips

Storm Short Wart

Match this aggressiveness with a faster retrieve to cover more water and catch more fish. Retrieve the bait quickly but steadily, occasionally snapping the rod tip to make the lure dart forward.

At the height of the prespawn period, it's virtually impossible to move a crankbait too fast for smallies to catch it. Reel as fast as you can while pumping the rod tip. The bait will rip forward in quick bursts and bounce erratically off the bottom and other structures. ☐

## Water Temperature and Spring Smallmouth Patterns

| Water Temperature (period) | Fish Location and Activity |
|---|---|
| 32°F to 39°F (Ice-out) | Deep (20 to 45 feet in deeper lakes; 12 to 20 feet in shallow lakes) transitions from harder to softer bottom intersecting basin flats off main-lake points, bars, and related humps. |
| 40°F to 42°F (Coldwater) | Same as above and halfway up the ends of points. |
| **43°F to 45°F (Late Coldwater)** | **The edge of flats and inside turns where deep water comes closest to shore on the same main-lake points.** |
| **46°F to 47°F (Early Prespawn)** | **A key transition period. Smallmouths make forays into shallow water, but most activity centers on inside turns and related rocks or secondary features along the primary drop-off.** |
| **48°F to 52°F (Mid-Prespawn)** | **Definite shallow movement. Beyond this point, most feeding activity is shallow. Weather permitting, activity levels soar.** |
| 53°F to 57°F (Late Prespawn) | Activity levels remain high to about 55°F, then taper. Fish scatter shallow. Docks, rocks, and other cover produce until the urge to spawn tempers feeding responses. |
| 58°F to 66°F (Spawn) | Nest building and egg laying. Females return quickly to deep water. Males continue to guard nests. |

# FLOAT TACTICS FOR STREAM SMALLMOUTHS

Floats are at their best when standard presentations like crankbaits and hair jigs fail. When you know fish are in the area but can't trigger them, drift a bait downstream beneath a float. It's the most natural and subtle way to tease small-mouths into taking, and it's also efficient. With a long rod and a few floats, a bait can be drifted 50, 100, even 150 feet, combing the water for fish. Smallies that won't move 2 feet to take a lure can't resist a bait suspended in front of their noses.

## When

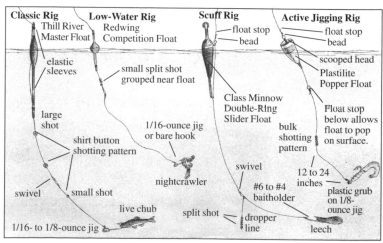

**Classic Rig**
Thill River Master Float
elastic sleeves
large shot
shirt button shotting pattern
swivel
small shot
live chub
1/16- to 1/8-ounce jig

**Low-Water Rig**
Redwing Competition Float
small split shot grouped near float
1/16-ounce jig or bare hook
nightcrawler

**Scuff Rig**
float stop
bead
Class Minnow Double-Ring Slider Float
swivel
#6 to #4 baitholder
split shot
dropper line

**Active Jigging Rig**
float stop
bead
scooped head
Plastilite Popper Float
bulk shotting pattern
Float stop below allows float to pop on surface.
12 to 24 inches
plastic grub on 1/8-ounce jig
leech

# Tackle

*Rod:* 7- to 10-foot fast-action medium-power spinning rod. *Reel:* medium-capacity spinning reel. *Line:* 6- to 8-pound-test mono.

# Rigging

For fixed floats, slide two silicone sleeves on the line—one for the top of the stem and one for the bottom. Insert the float into the sleeves. Tie a swivel to the line 6 to 12 inches below the float, then tie on a leader testing 2 pounds lighter than the main line. For slipfloats, place a neoprene float stop or stop knot and bead on the line followed by the float. Add enough shot to submerge two-thirds of the body of the float. Tie on a hook or plain jighead for livebait, or a small jig for active jigging. □

## *Stream Float Presentation*

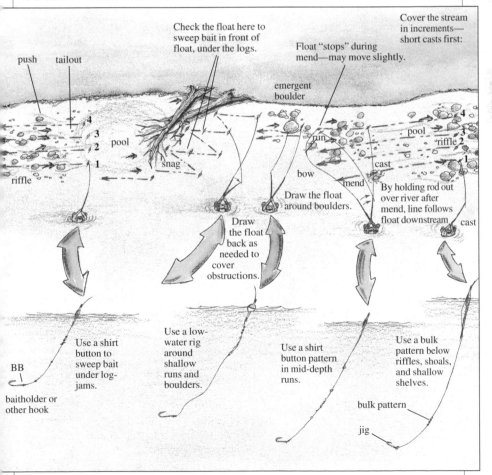

Check the float here to sweep bait in front of float, under the logs.

Float "stops" during mend—may move slightly.

Cover the stream in increments—short casts first:

push  tailout

emergent boulder

riffle  4  3  2  1  pool  snag  riffle  pool  run  cast  riffle  4  3  2  1

bow  mend  cast

Draw the float around boulders.

By holding rod out over river after mend, line follows float downstream  cast

Draw the float back as needed to cover obstructions.

Use a shirt button to sweep bait under log-jams.

Use a low-water rig around shallow runs and boulders.

Use a shirt button pattern in mid-depth runs.

Use a bulk pattern below riffles, shoals, and shallow shelves.

BB

baitholder or other hook

bulk pattern

jig

# MORE TUBE TRICKS FOR SMALLMOUTHS

It looks like nothing in particular, everything in general. A good fisherman sees a tube the way a sculptor sees a lump of clay. It becomes what the fisherman makes it. In the hands of an artist, it is transformed from a limp, frumpy, hollow piece of plastic into a dying shad; a bottom-crawling crawdad; a minnow suspending off bottom; a leech waving across the weed tops; a minnow fluttering on the surface; or something else a smallmouth might eat.

## Tackle

**Rod:** 6½- to 7½-foot medium- to medium-heavy-power fast-action spinning rod. **Reel:** medium-capacity spinning reel. **Line:** 6- to 10-pound monofilament.

## When

## Rigging

One of the characteristics that make tubes so effective is all the individual tail filaments quivering as the bait falls on a semi-tight line. Trimming off every other tail allows

**Bang Scent**

Bobby Garland's
Better Fishing
Ways Gitzit

Internal Weight Systems by
Eagle Claw and Hawg Buster

Alka Seltzer and
Florida-Rigged
Gambler Tube

Wazp Pulsator

Venom
Super Do

the tube to sink slightly faster on a 1/16-ounce head, while creating more vibration. A trimmed tube allows each of the remaining tails more room to move.

Some anglers prefer to use solid tubes for skipping under obstructions. A hard-bodied tube like the Venom Super Do or the Wazp Pulsator is more durable than softer baits. Skip the tube on a jighead under docks, piers, and overhanging willows on rivers, or any permanent structure that smallmouths might hold under.

Smallmouth guides on the Great Lakes also use solid tubes like the Super Do on small jigs in open water. Rig the tube so the solid paddle tail is horizontal to slow the fall rate and make the jig swim more erratically. These small-diameter baits also are great for post-cold-front conditions when smallmouth seem to prefer smaller offerings, but they're heavy enough to cast long distances.

Many anglers fish Alka Seltzer in a tube. Cut off a sliver of a tablet, slide it inside a Texas-rigged tube, and snug it into the belly of the hook. A trail of bubbles coming from the tube often is irresistible to a big smallie. Filling hollow tubes with scent may have a similar effect on reluctant fish.

Internal weight systems add another wrinkle. With the Eagle Claw system, the weight hangs on a wire clip near the eye of the L150G HP Hook. The Hawg Buster comes in one size, a 1/8-ouncer, which can be trimmed in half to create a 1/16-ounce head. It slips over the hook point, down the shank, and onto the bend near the eye. With either system, the weight is less likely to snag. □

# FINDING PRESPAWN SMALLMOUTHS

**O**nce smallmouths begin feeding in the shallows, the action jumps into high gear. While the first movements shallow are tentative, eventually the fish do much of their feeding there. Of course, weather remains a factor. Wind and extreme weather move fish into deeper water and reduce feeding. Aggressive shallow feeding also slows when the water broaches about 58°F, and smallies begin focusing on nesting.

## When

## Tackle

*Rod:* 6- to 6½-foot medium-power fast-action spinning rod. *Reel:* medium-capacity spinning reel. *Line:* 6- to 10-pound limp monofilament.

## Rigging

At the beginning of this period, few baits outperform jigs. Hair jigs tied on aspirin heads excel in rocky areas, since they hang less often in crevices than other designs. In sandy, weedy bays, try a 1/8- or 1/4-ounce Arky-style jig. A lead-shot tube rig, often effective on finicky fish, continues to produce until the water temperature approaches the low 50°F range, when suspending jerkbaits, small crankbaits, and in-line spinners come into play.

# Location

Smallmouths in lakes and reservoirs usually winter at 25 to 50 feet. Some fish, usually the biggest in the population, begin moving shallow under the ice. Increasing daylight cues movements into the shallows. Some biologists and veteran anglers speculate that water temperature has little effect on spring migrations.

Tracking studies indicate that the first movements from deep wintering lairs are to the base of mid-depth breaks near spawning habitat, in 17 to 28 feet of water. Some of these bass gradually work shallower, to the lip of the shallow flat in 8 to 10 feet of water. The route they follow often is a mirror image of the route they followed when leaving the shallows in fall.

Wind also positions fish. It creates current that pushes them into the farthest inside bend in a trough. On sandy shorelines, the trough closest to the bank draws smallmouths when the wind is blowing into the bank. Just because the surface temperature is in the 40°F range doesn't mean the fish won't be aggressive. □

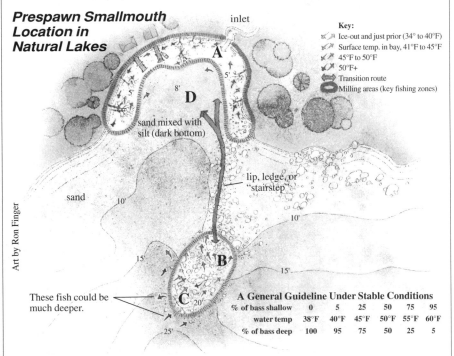

**Prespawn Smallmouth Location in Natural Lakes**

inlet

Key:
- Ice-out and just prior (34° to 40°F)
- Surface temp. in bay, 41°F to 45°F
- 45°F to 50°F
- 50°F+
- Transition route
- Milling areas (key fishing zones)

sand mixed with silt (dark bottom)

lip, ledge, or "stairstep"

sand

These fish could be much deeper.

Art by Ron Finger

**A General Guideline Under Stable Conditions**

| | | | | | | |
|---|---|---|---|---|---|---|
| % of bass shallow | 0 | 5 | 25 | 50 | 75 | 95 |
| water temp | 38°F | 40°F | 45°F | 50°F | 55°F | 60°F |
| % of bass deep | 100 | 95 | 75 | 50 | 25 | 5 |

**A.** Inlets into shallow bays (maximum depth 10 feet) are key indicators of spawning habitat.

**B.** The lip of the shallow flat, where it intersects the sharpest break into deep water is key—especially where rocks and boulders are present. Always check this spot.

**C.** Post-frontal fish generally locate here, at the base of the break in 15- to 20-foot depths.

**D.** Dark-bottom bays warm quickest and draw the most early activity after ice-out.

# SHORELINE CASTING AT NIGHT FOR WALLEYES

Walleyes possess a low-light vision advantage over many forms of prey. Perch that become inactive at sunset provide easy meals during the transition period between light and dark. Yet walleyes often continue feeding into the night, savaging shiners, ciscoes, shad, or other targets of opportunity. That doesn't mean they're not cautious; sudden unnatural sounds alert them to your presence, and they shut down or flee the area. If you're relatively stealthy, however, it's possible to catch them with their guard down.

**When**

## Tackle

*Rod:* 6½- to 7½-foot fast-action medium-power spinning rod. *Reel:* spinning reel with a long-cast spool. *Line:* 8- to 12-pound-test mono.

## Presentation

Whether you wade, fish from shore, fish from a boat, shorelines are the primary starting point for checking the nocturnal potential of a fishery. On lakes, rivers, or reservoirs, anywhere current enters or passes through narrows, crankbaits and jigs are prime methods for catching walleyes. Shallow-running crankbaits, in particular, are preferred since they're easy to carry and use—no fussing with livebait.

## Where In Reservoirs

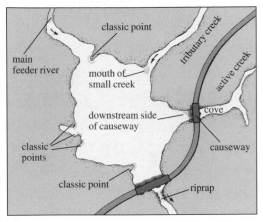

- classic point
- tributary creek
- main feeder river
- mouth of small creek
- active creek
- downstream side of causeway
- cove
- causeway
- classic points
- classic point
- riprap

Heavier versions cast a long distance into the darkness; lighter models are more subtle but offer a reduced range.

In general, minnow imitators dive only a foot or two and are ideal for skimming shallow rocks or weedtops. Use slow, steady retrieves. Particularly good are neutral buoyancy lures like Storm Suspending ThunderSticks or Normark Rapala Husky Jerks. Or make floating lures neutrally buoyant by placing adhesive Storm SuspenDots along the belly of the bait until it hangs motionless in the water. Creek mouths, piers, breakwalls, rock points, and other fish attractors are all good sites for pitching cranks.

Jigheads dressed with plastic tails back up crankbaits for a more bottom-oriented approach. Livebait generally isn't necessary; shad tails or twister tails entice strikes. Use steady retrieves to occasionally skim bottom. □

## Where In Rivers

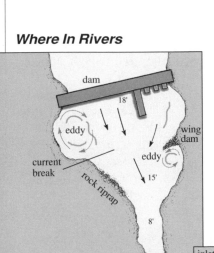

- dam
- 18'
- eddy
- wing dam
- current break
- rock riprap
- eddy
- 15'
- 8'
- bridge
- 10'
- incoming creek
- 3'
- 12'
- shallow rock bar adjacent to deep outside bend
- 10'
- shallow rock shoal adjacent to deep hole
- hole

## Where In Lakes

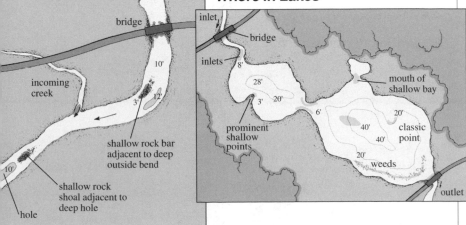

- inlet
- bridge
- inlets
- 8'
- 28'
- 3'
- 20'
- prominent shallow points
- 6'
- mouth of shallow bay
- 20'
- 40'
- classic point
- 40'
- 20'
- weeds
- outlet

# LIVEBAIT RIGGING FOR WALLEYES

Livebait rigs consist of hook, line, and sinker. What could be simpler? But sometimes, anything less than finesse won't do. Cold fronts send walleyes into hibernation, or at least reduce their enthusiasm for feeding. Fishing pressure makes them spooky—too many rigs dancing along the drop-off, too many of their buddies disappearing. Clear water accentuates the unnatural aspects of a poor presentation. Adjusting leader length, adding blades or beads for attraction, and using the best livebait are important factors in each situation.

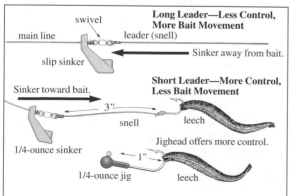

Deep Rigging—more vertical presentation.

15'

65'

8'

6'

Shallow Rigging—horizontal presentation with long line.

35'

## *Weight Placement Determines Control*

swivel

main line

leader (snell)

**Long Leader—Less Control, More Bait Movement**

slip sinker

Sinker away from bait.

Sinker toward bait.

**Short Leader—More Control, Less Bait Movement**

3"

snell

leech

1/4-ounce sinker

Jighead offers more control.

1"

1/4-ounce jig

leech

## When

The closer the weight is to your bait, the more control you have. A minnow, worm, or leech hooked on a jig is as close as you can bring a bait to a sinker, which is what the head of a jig is.

# Tackle

*Rod:* 6- to 7-foot medium-power spinning rod. *Reel:* medium-capacity spinning reel. *Line:* 6- to 10-pound-test mono.

# Presentation

When searching for active fish, start with a 18- to 24-inch leader, or a longer leader and a floating jighead. Move the bait along for about 15 feet and stop. Keep your line tight to the sinker while the minnow or leech struggles in place. Wait 10 seconds for following fish to tap the bait. If nothing happens, scoot along quickly for another 15 feet and stop. This approach with a 12-inch leader works in rivers for fish holding close to the bottom.

Generally, the deeper the water the more vertically you should fish a rig. In water shallower than 6 feet, use a cast-troll presentation. Position your boat over deep water upwind from the structural element and cast toward the shallows. Troll with the same move-stop approach at an angle to the shallow portion of the bar until the bait moves into deep water. Reel in, cast again, and troll for another 80 or so feet. If you find fish, anchor and cast. □

## *Rigging Options*

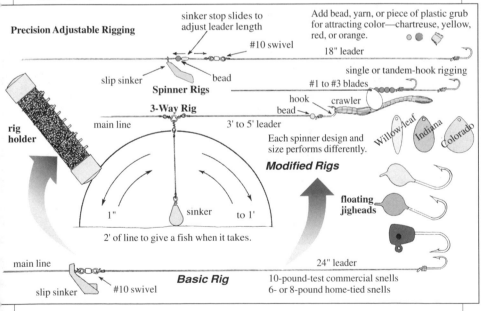

Precision Adjustable Rigging

sinker stop slides to adjust leader length

#10 swivel

slip sinker       bead

**Spinner Rigs**

**3-Way Rig**

rig holder

main line          3' to 5' leader

1"       sinker      to 1'

2' of line to give a fish when it takes.

Add bead, yarn, or piece of plastic grub for attracting color—chartreuse, yellow, red, or orange.

18" leader

single or tandem-hook rigging

#1 to #3 blades

hook   crawler
bead

Each spinner design and size performs differently.

Willow-leaf   Indiana   Colorado

**Modified Rigs**

floating jigheads

main line          24" leader

slip sinker   #10 swivel

**Basic Rig**

10-pound-test commercial snells
6- or 8-pound home-tied snells

31

# PLANER BOARD TROLLING FOR WALLEYES

**P**laner board trolling incorporates a blend of traditional longline trolling with precision depth coverage, eliminating vast areas of unproductive water to zero in on sections that hold fish. Planers take lines and lures out to the sides of the boat, allowing anglers to cover a wider trolling swath, simultaneously run multiple baits, and minimize

spooking fish in clear or shallow water. It's particularly effective when walleyes are moving between areas. At other times, fish may be attracted to a general area by structural features like points, humps, islands, or channels, but they suspend when they're not relating to the structure itself. Any time walleyes roam the basin, down and out trolling tactics can score big.

## When

## Tackle

*Rod:* 7½- to 8-foot medium-power casting rod with a parabolic action.
*Reel:* large-capacity baitcasting or line-counting reel with a smooth drag.
*Line:* 10-pound-test monofilament or fused polyethylene line.

## Rigging

In-line planers clamp onto line with one or more release clips. Run your lure behind the boat at a slow trolling speed until it reaches the desired distance, then

### Fishing High And Low

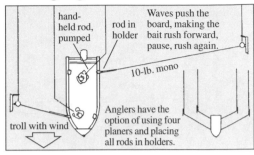

hand-
held rod,
pumped

rod in
holder

Waves push the
board, making the
bait rush forward,
pause, rush again.

10-lb. mono

troll with wind

Anglers have the
option of using four
planers and placing
all rods in holders.

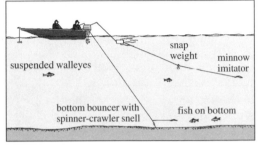

snap
weight

minnow
imitator

suspended walleyes

bottom bouncer with
spinner-crawler snell

fish on bottom

engage the reel. Add a snap weight with a pinch-on clip 50 feet ahead of the lure for fishing deeper than the lure can run on its own. Next, clamp the planer to the line, selecting a left or right model depending on which side of the boat you want to run your line. Lower the planer into the water with the rod and disengage the reel. A slow trolling speed creates enough drag to pull line off the reel and angle the planer off to the side of the boat. Once it reaches the desired distance, engage the reel and set the rod in a rod holder.

# Presentation

Strikes aren't always obvious, so watch your boards carefully. Sometimes the planer bobs and weaves, dropping back when a big fish hits your lure. Other times, the board barely lags or rocks as a hooked fish swims along with the boat. When a fish hits, shift the engine into neutral. Take the rod out of the holder and begin slowly reeling in. Don't pump the rod. Your drag should be set light enough to slip under fairly light tension. Continue reeling until you can reach the board, then pop it off the line. Follow the same procedure with your snap weight. Then land the fish. □

### Weighting Systems

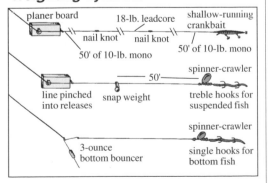

planer board

18-lb. leadcore

shallow-running
crankbait

nail knot    nail knot

50' of 10-lb. mono

50' of 10-lb. mono

50'

spinner-crawler

line pinched
into releases

snap weight

treble hooks for
suspended fish

spinner-crawler

3-ounce
bottom bouncer

single hooks for
bottom fish

# FISHING RIVER DUNES FOR WALLEYES

Traditional wisdom suggests to avoid long straight river stretches of shallow or consistent depth during spring, moving instead from hole to hole. That's where most of the fish should be. But walleyes have to get from point A to point B, and quickly moving in a straight line may not be their best option. Given the chance, they will likely stop to rest somewhere along the way, rather than fighting current in one continuous sprint.

## When

## Tackle

*Rod:* 6- to 6½-foot medium-power spinning rod. *Reel:* spinning reel with a medium-capacity spool. *Line:* 6- or 8-pound mono.

## Location

Long straight river stretches may appear featureless, but if walleyes can find some form of current break, even if it's subtle and shallow, they often use it to break up their sprint between holes. An area of rolling sand dunes is a classic example—one few anglers realize exists. At some point, the bottom begins to roll, with sand pushed by current eventually forming a network of significant peaks and valleys several feet high.

These dunes often are associated with one shoreline, while most of the current extends from midriver to the opposite bank. Walleyes dodge from valley to valley, briefly tucking into the valleys to escape the brunt of the flow, and perhaps to feed. Then it's off again to the next major bend.

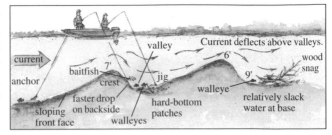

# Rigging

Experiment with jig weight to match depth and current, allowing your jig to tumble or roll along the bottom at an effective pace to trigger strikes. That could be a slow drift, a series of lifts and pauses, or an extended rest in place. Once you determine the mood of the fish, fine-tune with other factors like sound, vibration, bulk, profile, scent, and color to entice additional bites.

# Presentation

The easiest way to fish a dune area is to make casts of different lengths at about 90 degrees to either side of the boat, engage your reel, and let the jig tumble and roll across bottom, moving downcurrent in an arc to a position directly downstream. Grip the line with your index finger to help sense strikes. Raise the rod tip a bit to lift the jig off bottom, should it come to rest, then lower it. The current does the rest.

To cover more area for active fish, make the same casts, let the jig fall to bottom, but don't engage the reel. Instead, grip the line with your index finger and let the jig roll a few feet. Then release your finger and pop the rod tip upward, stripping off 3 to 6 feet of line. Regrasp and redrift. Repeat. Follow the direction of the drift by pointing your rod tip at the jig. Done properly, drifting a bigger area is possible, though the jig tends to move quickly, and you lose control at a distance. □

## *Different Degrees of Action and Attraction*

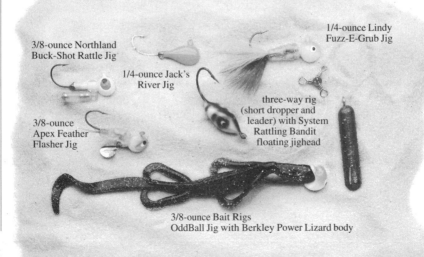

3/8-ounce Northland Buck-Shot Rattle Jig

1/4-ounce Jack's River Jig

1/4-ounce Lindy Fuzz-E-Grub Jig

3/8-ounce Apex Feather Flasher Jig

three-way rig (short dropper and leader) with System Rattling Bandit floating jighead

3/8-ounce Bait Rigs OddBall Jig with Berkley Power Lizard body

# ICE-OUT STRATEGIES FOR SAUGEYE

Talk spring saugeyes and most anglers think shallow, think shoreline, think twilight. Think again. Until the water darkens, saugeyes may be reluctant to move shallow and instead may be fish of the extreme depths. Thus it takes a versatile approach to catch them consistently throughout the transition from the Spring Coldwater Period to the Spawn Period. Tactics change with location, and the better you have 'em wired, the more fish you'll catch.

## When

## Tackle

**Rods:** 6-foot medium-power spinning rod for vertical jigging and 6- to 8-foot spinning or casting rods for crankbait trolling. **Reels:** medium-capacity spinning or baitcasting reels. **Line:** 6- or 8-pound limp monofilament for jigging and 10-pound abrasion-resistant line for trolling.

## Rigging

The key to effective riprap trolling is to stagger lines and lures at different depths to cover the sloping face of a dam or causeway. Select lures that run at a range of depths. Troll the shallowest baits closest to the dam, switching to deeper-running cranks farther out. Use different rod lengths to spread lines on the same side of the boat.  Do likewise on the opposite side of the boat, but consider the slope of the rock face and the lure's running depth to reach near or occasionally bounce bottom.

## Location & Presentation

While saugeyes are known for night activity in the shallows and shallow daytime feeding if the water is muddy, clearer water right at ice-out may keep them deep for a while.  That's the light-sensitive sauger side of their personality.  Vertically jigging or livebait rigging the tips of deep structure near a dam or the deep hole below a dam may be your best daytime location until the water warms and darkens.

Soon after ice-out, warming water and run-off cloud the water and reduce light penetration, eventually drawing saugeyes shallow.  Much like walleyes, they move to shallow rock structure, feeding primarily at night, but also during the day if the water's muddy.  Cast or longline troll shallow-running minnow-imitators or shad crankbaits as parallel to shore as possible.  The fish could be in as little as 1 to 3 feet of water, so don't cast or troll too deep.  Shorecasting conditions near dams are excellent, with easy foot access to prime spots.  ☐

## A Day and Night Difference

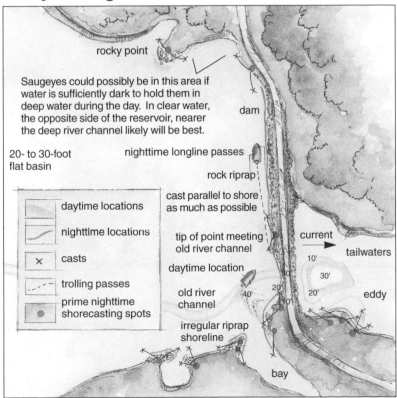

rocky point

Saugeyes could possibly be in this area if water is sufficiently dark to hold them in deep water during the day. In clear water, the opposite side of the reservoir, nearer the deep river channel likely will be best.

dam

20- to 30-foot flat basin

nighttime longline passes

rock riprap

cast parallel to shore as much as possible

| | daytime locations |
| | nighttime locations |
| × | casts |
| | trolling passes |
| • | prime nighttime shorecasting spots |

tip of point meeting old river channel

daytime location

old river channel

irregular riprap shoreline

current

tailwaters

10'

30'

20'

40'

30'

20'

10'

eddy

bay

# SWIMMING JIGS FOR WEEDLINE CRAPPIES

In summer, though crappies often disperse to many locations, most use the weedline at one time or another. Some use pockets in deep cabbage beds all summer, while those in open water are blown onto weedlines where wind-driven plankton blooms pile in, following consecutive days of winds from the same direction. The schools use shallow and mid-depth weed flats all summer, moving to the weedlines and beyond during bright days or inclement weather.

## When

## Tackle

*Rod:* 6½- to 7-foot fast-action light-power rod. *Reel:* medium-capacity spinning reel with long-cast spool. *Line:* 4- or 6-pound limp monofilament.

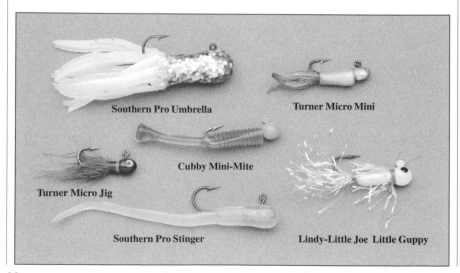

Southern Pro Umbrella

Turner Micro Mini

Cubby Mini-Mite

Turner Micro Jig

Southern Pro Stinger

Lindy-Little Joe Little Guppy

# Location

In a typical summer scenario in lakes and reservoirs with well-developed weed-lines, crappies that use weedlines on a daily or almost daily basis suspend between 12 and 20 feet below the surface during the day, moving up to the weedline to feed during low-light periods of dawn and dusk.

It's common to see crappies on the surface just after the sun goes down or just before it rises, especially if an insect hatch is underway. Actually, spotting crappies isn't necessary for identification. If the rising fish makes a distinct sound like a bubble being burst or leaves a big bubble in the middle of the rise, it's a crappie.

As the sun climbs, surface activity diminishes. Tube jigs or jigs and minnows might be the optimum choice early or late in the day, but casting and swimming small tubes or other plastic options covers water more efficiently. Few fish can be seen on sonar, making it critical to continually probe different depths.

# Presentation

Two types of lift-drop retrieves are made in a different manner for different conditions, but both create the same basic jig action. On calm water, cast, raise the rod tip to about 10:30, and count the jig down to the desired depth ("one thousand, two thousand . . ." about one second per half foot). Reel down to 9:30, then lift the rod tip back to 10:30, making the jig ride, rise, and fall at a consistent depth. Watch the line for strikes.

On windy days when line watching is less effective, use your finger to detect hits. Cast and bring the rod tip down to 9:00 as you count the jig down. Engage the reel and leave your trigger finger on the line. At the desired depth, bring the rod tip to 10:00. After a brief pause, again raise the rod tip to 11:00, then 12:00, then quickly reel down to 9:00 and start over.

A nodding retrieve is made with the rod tip held high. Cast and count the jig down as you raise the rod tip to 11:00. Wrist action moves the rod tip only slightly—from 11:00 to 11:30. Raise the rod tip slowly, then reel back to 11:00. The result is a slow roller-coaster undulation that keeps the jig at the desired depth. □

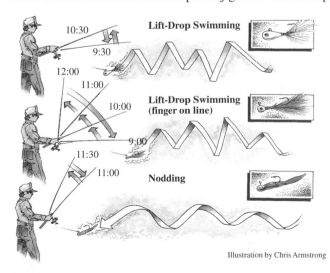

10:30    **Lift-Drop Swimming**

9:30

12:00

11:00

10:00    **Lift-Drop Swimming (finger on line)**

9:00

11:30

11:00    **Nodding**

Illustration by Chris Armstrong

# NIGHT BITE CRAPPIES

Many crappie anglers concentrate on spring pre-spawn and spawning fish in shallow coves and creek arms. As male crappies guard hatching fry, females disperse toward open water. Males follow as soon as their parental duties are complete. But as fishing pressure on crappies increases, most anglers continue to ignore an important fact—throughout most of the season, night is the best time to catch crappies. These bug-eyed predators see well after dark and take advantage of nocturnal prey movements to feed efficiently.

## When

## Tackle

*Rod:* 6- to 7-foot light-power spinning rod. *Reel:* small-capacity spinning reel. *Line:* 4- to 8-pound-test mono.

## Rigging

Livebait or jigs suspended below slip floats are effective night rigs. Tie a stop knot on your main line, followed by a bead and a small, narrow slipfloat. The float should be sensitive enough to balance with a few small shot so it can easily be pulled under by a light-biting crappie. Light-wire #6 to #1 hooks keep small minnows alive and active, and they hook crappies firmly. Popular baits vary by region, but fathead minnows are tough to beat for numbers of fish. Use medium-size shiners to attract large crappies.

# Location

At night, crappies move toward the surface and gather to feed below schools of baitfish. Find a concentration of active crappies at night, and you'll experience some of the finest fishing in freshwater. Large main-lake points and the mouths of large creeks often attract large schools of shad and crappies. Bridges are another good area to intercept nocturnal crappies. The riprapped banks, old abutments, and lights associated with bridges attract plankton and baitfish, and in turn, crappies. On populated lakes, lighted docks also attract crappies and their prey. In clear water, docks standing in at least five feet of water produce best, while crappies in murky water often move much shallower.

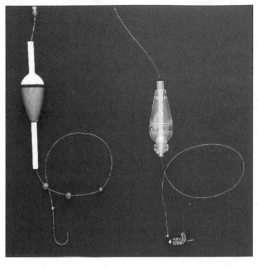

# Presentation

Once you locate crappies, catching them isn't difficult. Slowly cruising around an area while watching your electronics often reveals the presence of crappies and their forage. Set your float stop to suspend your bait slightly above the fish and cast into the fray. If the action stops during the night, check the area with sonar or adjust your stop knot before moving to another spot. Shad and other baitfish often follow clouds of plankton by making vertical movements throughout the night, and crappies likely follow. ☐

## *Boat Docks*

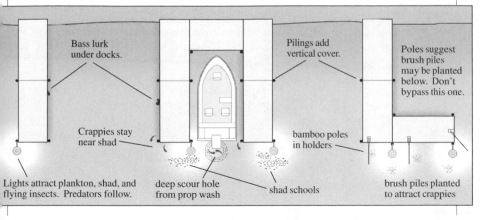

Bass lurk under docks.

Pilings add vertical cover.

Poles suggest brush piles may be planted below. Don't bypass this one.

Crappies stay near shad

bamboo poles in holders

Lights attract plankton, shad, and flying insects. Predators follow.

deep scour hole from prop wash

shad schools

brush piles planted to attract crappies

# FINDING POSTSPAWN BLUEGILLS

**B**luegills spawn when water temperature ranges from about 67°F to 74°F; then they scatter. Males may linger near spawning habitat for a few days, but females move quickly into postspawn patterns. They may suspend over deep water, following wind-driven plankton. Or, more often, they inhabit both shallow and deep weedlines, rock piles, or humps. Finding a few bluegills is seldom a problem, but finding concentrations—especially big fish—is a matter of keying on prime postspawn patterns.

## When

## Tackle

***Rod:*** 5- to 7-foot light-power spinning rod. ***Reel:*** lightweight spinning reel with long-cast spool. ***Line:*** 2- to 6-pound-test limp mono. □

**Understanding postspawn behavior is the key to finding concentrations of big 'gills during summer.**

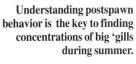

## Summer Bluegill Patterns

Spawning (67°F to 74°F) often takes place in areas of slightly harder bottom. Larger 'gills may spawn in deeper water. In clear water, 'gills may spawn 8 to 12 feet down.

| | |
|---|---|
| ⬚ | bluegills |
| ⬚ | pads |
| ⬚ | cabbage-coontail beds |
| ⬚ | sparse cabbage on hard bottom |
| ⬚ | rock |
| ⬚ | junk weed |

Deep pads attract some fish.

37'

hard-bottom hump

27'

By midsummer to late summer, some of the biggest bluegills migrate to main-lake weedlines, points, and humps. The best main-lake locations generally are near fertile bays or part of the most fertile segment of the lake— fertile meaning they offer soft bottom and weedgrowth.

After spawning (+74°F) big bluegills migrate to deep weedlines and offshore humps.

When forage thins along deep weedlines, some bluegills suspend, following windblown clouds of plankton (midsummer, usually over 72°F).

15'

### Summer Period (70°F to 82°F)

⬅ wind

lowlight periods

plankton

Three major patterns:
• deep weedlines
• rocky humps (or weed humps in deep water)
• suspended fish following windblown plankton

suspended fish

deep rockpile

12'

daytime

25'

# ICING YELLOW PERCH

In the water, yellow perch are a challenge, especially jumbos weighing a pound or more. On the table, they're perfection. And they're fun to catch, too. The problem is finding them. Yellow perch are opportunists—some may hold near rock and gravel, while others are on sand or muck; some may be deep, while others are shallow. Perch usually relate to the bottom, but they also suspend. Perch also love to hold near weedgrowth. With so many options available to the fish, focus on high-percentage spots and keep moving until you contact concentrations of fish.

## When

*Lures For Aggressive Perch In Deep Water*

Left to right:
Bay de Noc Do-
Jigger, Bay de Noc
Swedish Pimple,
Northland Fire-Eye
Minnow, Jigging
Rapala, Acme
Kastmaster

## Tackle

*Rod:* 2- to 3-foot ultralight fast-action ice rod. *Reel:* small-capacity spinning reel. *Line:* 4-pound-test mono.

## Rigging

Bigger and bolder is better to attract and then trigger perch in deep water. The depths are darker, so fish can't discriminate detail so well, and they aren't so harassed as fish in shallow water. These

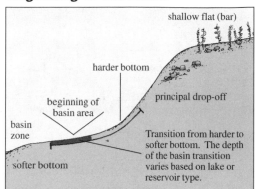

**Beginning Of The Basin**

shallow flat (bar)

harder bottom

beginning of basin area

principal drop-off

basin zone

softer bottom

Transition from harder to softer bottom. The depth of the basin transition varies based on lake or reservoir type.

deep fish often are difficult to find, but relatively easy to catch with a handful of proven lures. Flash lures like 1/8- to 1/4-ounce jigging spoons, or swimming lures like a #3 or #5 Jigging Rapala, are the best choice when perch are aggressive. Tip the treble hook with maggots or a minnow head. When perch are picky, switch to a search lure like Custom Jigs and Spins' Slip Dropper rig tipped with 3 or 4 maggots. Make your own search lure by replacing the treble hook on a jigging spoon with 2½ inches of 4-pound-test line and a tiny jig.

## Location

Perch prefer ranging on flats and tend not to hold on drop-offs. Once perch slide off shallow flats, they usually drop all the way to the base of the drop-off, and range in the area of the drop-off—particularly in the section where the transition from harder to softer bottom begins. This transition usually occurs within 50 yards of the base of the drop-off. Target the 100-yard zone beginning at the base of the drop-off and running into the basin.

Perch often roam in groups that may cover several hundred yards and include hundreds or even thousands of fish. It's not difficult to find them, however, if you search systematically. A group of three anglers, for example, can quickly search a large area by drilling holes perpendicular to the basin edge. Drop a bait down to the bottom, do some aggressive jigging, and watch your electronics for signs of fish. Give a hole three minutes, then move further down the edge.

## Presentation

Aggressive jigging, that is, quick lift-falls of a foot or more, attract fish—bring them in for a closer look at the bait. Watch for fish on sonar. When a fish moves in, jiggle the rod tip so the jig quivers in place, then stop. When the fish moves in closer, give another little jiggle and stop again. Often fish in deep water will immediately move in and inhale the bait. If there's any hesitation, slowly jiggle the bait as you raise it a couple inches. If the fish still refuses to take, resume aggressive jigging to call in another fish. □

# BULLHEADS DURING SPRING

**B**ullheads are the first fish caught by many anglers. Prized by children, but often forgotten or at least overlooked by fishermen who pursue more "serious" species. Bullheads will never be the stuff of bass tournaments, expensive advertising campaigns, and high-tech gadgets. Bullheads are just plain bullheads and that's good enough. Whether on the line or in the pan, they possess a magic we never outgrow.

## When

## Tackle

*Rod:* 6- to 7½-foot medium-power spinning rod. *Reel:* medium-capacity spinning reel. *Line:* 8- to 12-pound-test mono.

## Rigging

The same set and float rigs used for catfish catch bullheads, but leadhead jigs may be the best option. Choose a jig with a 1/0 or 2/0 hook, and add a nightcrawler or two. Thread worms onto the hook loosely, leaving the hook point exposed and the head of the crawler free to wriggle. Bullheads eat down to the leadhead and then have a difficult time swallowing it. By then you have 'em. The head of the jig also makes a good handle for unhooking fish. Stand-up jigs with wedge heads work best.

## Location

In spring, bullheads are drawn to warmer water and more abundant food in backwater areas. In the lake illustrated here, bullheads from the main body of

## The Best Jigheads

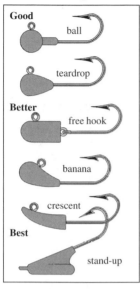

**Good**
- ball
- teardrop

**Better**
- free hook
- banana

- crescent

**Best**
- stand-up

**Leadhead jigs filled with worms and fished stationary on the bottom are great for bullheads.**

## Concentration Spots

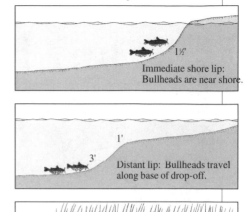

1½'
Immediate shore lip: Bullheads are near shore.

1'
3'
Distant lip: Bullheads travel along base of drop-off.

2'
Weed lip: Bullheads travel along front face of weeds.

water move through the connecting canal into the backwater. Once in the backwater, some of them move into the slough—primarily black bullhead territory. Yellow and and brown bullheads usually remain in the backwater. A reverse migration occurs after the spawn. Some black bullheads, though, may remain in the backwater throughout summer if current prevents excessive water stagnation.

Bullheads often concentrate in funnel areas like **Canals A** and **B**. Bullheads must move thorough these areas, and current tends to concentrate washed in food to attract and hold them. Vegetation breaks like the bulrushes along the north and south shorelines of the backwater also gather fish. Bullheads travel the front face of these spots, but tend to concentrate where vegetation stops (**C, D, E**, and **F**) and where it forms points. Areas immediately outside **Canal A** attract bullheads after they spawn. Fish the front face of reeds and cabbage, plus the coontail flats and the outside edge of the deeper weeds. □

### Backwater Bullheads

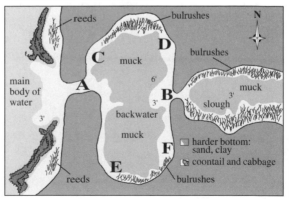

reeds
bulrushes
N
**D**
bulrushes
**C**  muck
6'
main body of water
**A**  **B**
3'  slough
muck
backwater
3'  muck
□ harder bottom: sand, clay
**F**
▨ coontail and cabbage
**E**
reeds  bulrushes

# DIPBAIT RIGGING FOR CHANNEL CATS

**D**ipbaits usually are the tool of choice among the hardcore catfish anglers who fish with commercially prepared baits. Dips are creamy—just thin enough to require a delivery vehicle—usually a plastic worm, but sometimes a piece of sponge or a two-inch length of surgical tubing with holes. Stir the bait to the right consistency, dab a dry worm around in the bait, dip the worm in water to lock the bait on the worm, and you're ready to catch cats. Provided, of course, that the rest of your rigging is suited to the situation.

## When

## Tackle

*Rod:* 6½- to 7½-foot spinning or casting rod. *Reel:* medium-capacity spinning or baitcasting reel. *Line:* 10- to 15-pound monofilament.

# Rigging

Whether you're after cats in lakes, rivers, or reservoirs, keep your rigging as simple as possible. For river fishing, just add a lead shot or two several inches above the dip worm. Resist placing the shot too far up your line because it becomes more difficult to cast and increases snagging.

The most popular rigging consists of an egg sinker sliding on the main line above a small snap swivel. Vary the size of the egg sinker, based on current and

## Rigging Options For Dip Worms

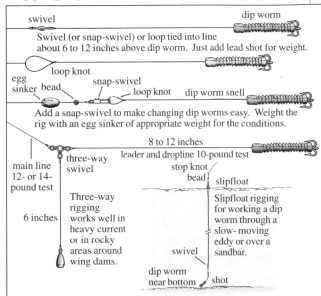

swivel
dip worm
Swivel (or snap-swivel) or loop tied into line about 6 to 12 inches above dip worm. Just add lead shot for weight.

loop knot
egg sinker bead
snap-swivel
loop knot
dip worm snell
Add a snap-swivel to make changing dip worms easy. Weight the rig with an egg sinker of appropriate weight for the conditions.

8 to 12 inches
leader and dropline 10-pound test
main line 12- or 14-pound test
three-way swivel
stop knot
bead
slipfloat

6 inches
Three-way rigging works well in heavy current or in rocky areas around wing dams.

Slipfloat rigging for working a dip worm through a slow- moving eddy or over a sandbar.

swivel
dip worm near bottom
shot

how far you need to cast. A 4mm bead between the sinker and the snap swivel protects the knot from the sliding sinker.

A dip worm snell should run about 6 inches to no more than about 12 inches. Tie a loop knot on the end of the snell. Slip the loop onto the snag portion of the snap swivel. Changing worms is easy if a fish swallows the bait or if you want to try a different worm style. Have at least a dozen worms rigged and ready before you hit the water.

Three-way rigging works well on big rivers, particularly around rocky habitat like wing dams. Tie your main line to one rung of a three-way swivel, then add a 6- to 12-inch dropper to another rung. Add a bell sinker of appropriate weight to the drop line. The dip snell should be 3 or 4 inches longer than the dropper.

Floats also work, particularly in rivers where slower-moving water runs through an eddy or pool. Keep the bait ticking along bottom as the float pulls it downstream. A slipfloat makes depth adjustment easier as the bottom changes.

## Presentation

Cats take a dip worm by arching down on the worm from slightly above as it rests on the bottom. A big fish often grabs a bait on the first bite, while a smaller fish tests it a time or two before taking it into its mouth. Don't set too quickly when cats are pecking at the bait.

When a fish has the bait, your rod tip will start to move away. Often the cat hooks itself, but set the hook anyway, and reel in the fish. A needle-nose pliers is handy for removing small treble hooks. Better yet, use the pliers to pinch down the hook barbs before you start to fish, or replace those trebles with #2 single hooks. □

# BRIDGES FOR EARLY-SEASON CHANNEL CATS

**C**urrent draws catfish during most of the year, but particularly during the Prespawn Period. That's obvious to anglers who fish rivers, but not always obvious on ponds, lakes, and reservoirs. Current attracts and concentrates forage. And food is of primary concern for channel cats that have shifted into a fourth-gear feeding frenzy.

## When

## Rigging

A variety of baits work during prime time. Dipbait becomes more effective as the season progresses. Having at least one natural bait along is always a good idea, too. Crawlers can be good in some situations, especially when the water is high during spring. And fresh cutbait always is productive. Cut 4- or 5-inch shiners into one-inch cubes, or fillet the sides off larger baitfish like suckers or gizzard shad and cut them into one-inch strips.

# Location

Bridges often aren't the best places to fish in rivers, but in lakes and reservoirs bridges are built over necked areas. Sometimes these narrows connect one lake with another, other times they connect two portions of the lake. Bridges mean current, current attracts and concentrates forage, and forage means catfish.

Bridge areas that connect shallow areas with deeper areas are particularly productive. Could be a marsh area on one side of the bridge connected to the main lake. Catfish hold in the main lake during winter, but are drawn to the current from the warm runoff coming from the marsh beginning in early spring. Usually the current flows from the marsh into the main lake, so most of the cats hold on the main-lake side of the bridge.

Another good spot is where a bridge crosses a creek near where it runs into a lake or reservoir. In creeks with good catfish habitat, a bridge isn't necessarily the key to finding catfish, because once cats begin migrating up the creek, they can be found in many areas. Most bridges, though, are built over riffle areas because the bottom is hard. So when a bridge is built over a stream near where it

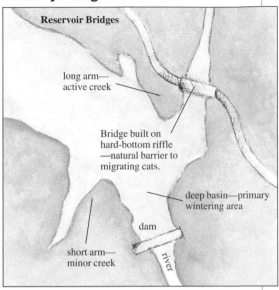

Reservoir Bridges

long arm— active creek

Bridge built on hard-bottom riffle —natural barrier to migrating cats.

deep basin—primary wintering area

dam

river

short arm— minor creek

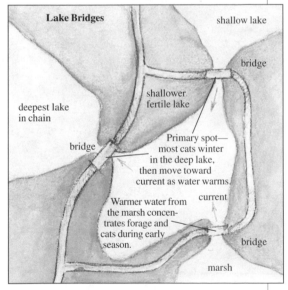

Lake Bridges

shallow lake

bridge

deepest lake in chain

shallower fertile lake

bridge

Primary spot— most cats winter in the deep lake, then move toward current as water warms.

current

Warmer water from the marsh concentrates forage and cats during early season.

bridge

marsh

dumps into a reservoir, it usually blocks the progress of cats migrating upstream.

Perhaps the best bridge spots connect major parts of lakes or reservoirs. If the system contains several such bridges, the best usually connects the deepest lake with the next lake in the chain. Most of the channel cats hold in the deep lake during winter, so the first bridge is the major traffic area when cats move into the shallower lakes during spring. These bridges can be productive during fall, too, since cats migrate back into the deep lake from the shallower lakes. □

# FINDING EARLY-SEASON FLATHEADS IN BIG RIVERS

**B**ig Rivers intimidate catmen accustomed to the intimacy of smaller streams. The transition from a small river with visible riffles and holes to a wide and deep river like the Mississippi, Ohio, Missouri, or Tennessee may seem overwhelming. But study a manageable stretch of water and you'll likely see many similarities to your favorite catfish river. A hole may be 50 feet deep instead of 10, and 500 yards long instead of 20, but that's just a matter of scale. Narrowing your search to the most productive areas is the key to locating flatheads.

## When

## Tackle

*Rod:* 6- to 8-foot heavy-power casting rod. *Reel:* large-capacity baitcasting reel. *Line:* 30- to 60-pound abrasion-resistant monofilament.

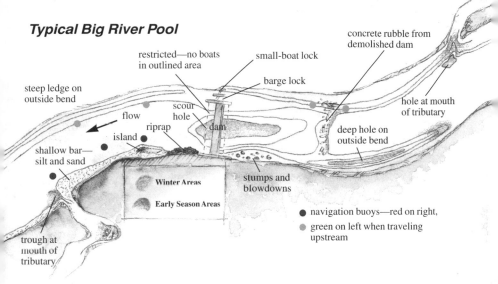

**Typical Big River Pool**

steep ledge on outside bend

restricted—no boats in outlined area

small-boat lock

barge lock

concrete rubble from demolished dam

flow

scour hole

riprap

dam

hole at mouth of tributary

island

deep hole on outside bend

shallow bar— silt and sand

**Winter Areas**

stumps and blowdowns

**Early Season Areas**

navigation buoys—red on right, green on left when traveling upstream

trough at mouth of tributary

# Location

Once water temperatures climb into the low- to mid-50°F range, which often coincides with heavy spring rains, flatheads begin feeding heavily. Wintering holes offer plenty of security and comfort, but little food, so cats begin seeking areas that concentrate forage species. Large minnows, shad, and any other fish species of appropriate size and abundance—from white suckers to white bass—are important prey. Increasing river current forces baitfish to hold behind shoreline snags, wing dams, and in holes on outside bends.

*Deep Structure:* Flatheads won't move far from wintering holes if sufficient forage is available nearby. The best wintering areas provide depth and protection from current. The lower third of a typical big river pool usually harbors the deepest and slackest holes. Begin your early-season search in this section, near the main river channel, surveying the bottom with sonar for structural elements that provide cover and deflect current.

*Shoreline Barriers:* By midspring, heavy run-off often makes anchoring in the main channel or presenting baits in deep water difficult. In fast water, look for shoreline bars on inside bends or at creek mouths. While the current in the middle of the river is fast, water traveling outside the main channel is slowed by friction with the bottom. These areas also provide cover that attracts and holds baitfish.

*Tributary Mouths:* The mouths of large tributary streams also act as barriers. Large deltas may partially block the flow of the main river, creating a lakelike environment with little current upstream. These areas also concentrate baitfish that eventually spawn in the smaller rivers. Flatheads hold in the slack water of the tributary mouth, gorging on shad and other forage. □

# TAILWATER STRATEGIES FOR BLUE CATS

The urge to procreate draws blue catfish to tailwaters. As days grow longer and the water warms, they leave deep wintering holes and begin moving upstream toward spawning areas. Before dams were built, the only structures that interrupted this annual procession were natural barriers like shoals and logjams. Today, however, runs usually are stopped short by dams.

## When

## Tackle

*Rod:* 6½- to 8-foot heavy-power casting rod. *Reel:* large-capacity baitcasting reel. *Line:* 30- to 60-pound abrasion-resistant monofilament.

## Rigging

Chunks of cutbait usually are most productive. Slice a shad, herring, or sucker into one-inch chunks, since larger pieces may be difficult to present properly in swift current. Push the hook once through the bait, leaving the point exposed to ensure a good hookset.

# Location

To better understand the dynamics of a tailwater, we divide the tailwater into three sections: the whitewater reach, which is the uppermost portion of the tailwater near the dam and adjacent structures; the middle reach, which begins where churning water from the dam begins smoothing out and slowing down; and the downstream reach, which begins where manmade structures are replaced by natural habitat.

*The Whitewater Reach:* From late spring through summer, this section of the tailwater serves up the best action for trophy blues. Current velocity, baitfish abundance, and oxygen content reach their highest levels here—conditions big blues like. As upstream spawning migrations progress, catfish crowd into the food-rich water immediately below the dam in ever-increasing numbers, with larger fish laying claim to prime feeding locations.

*The Middle Reach:* Moving downstream from the washout hole, we enter the middle reach, a stretch of calmer water where manmade structures such as dikes and riprap still are prevalent. A few blue cats, especially smaller fish, inhabit this section throughout the warm months, but trophy action peaks during short periods of reduced water flow through the dam. If one or several gates are closed, blue cats feeding in the whitewater reach often move to middle-reach structures that attract schools of baitfish and other forage.

*The Downstream Reach:* Eventually, the river becomes natural again. The channel begins meandering once more, trees have toppled in, cutbanks reappear, and the hand of man is less evident. This is the downstream reach of the tailwater. Blue cats pass through this area during upstream and downstream migrations, and also if conditions in the whitewater reach become unfavorable for extended periods in late spring and summer. □

### Tailwater Hot Spots

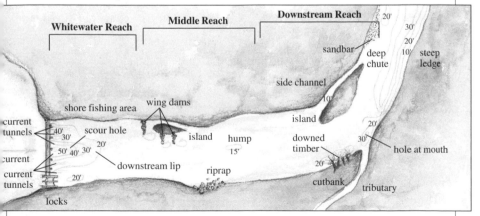

# CIRCLE HOOKS FOR CATFISH

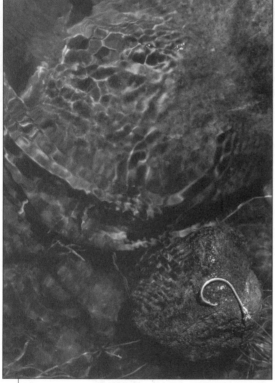

Circle hooks can't be set like standard hooks. Instead, a fish drives the hook home on its own as it pulls steadily away from an anchored line. That's the reason circle hooks work so well on limblines and log-lines for catfish or on long-lines for sailfish, halibut, and other saltwater species—no meddling angler to pull the hook away from the fish.

After the fish engulfs the baited hook and begins to move away, the hook slides up the gullet and along the inside of the mouth without catching. Once the eye of the hook clears the corner of the mouth, though, the hook rotates and the point begins to penetrate the soft tissue at the corner of the fishes jaw. As the fish continues to struggle, the point penetrates past the barb and the fish rarely escapes.

## Presentation

The most difficult task for rod and reel catmen is resisting the urge to drive the hook home when a cat picks up the bait. Instead, apply steady pressure by pointing the rod tip at the fish and reeling in slack line. When the line tightens and the point catches the inside corner of the cat's mouth, the rod tip can be lifted firmly, but never sharply. A standard hookset, as my initial experience shows, only pulls the hook from the fish's mouth.

Circle hooks are a natural choice for channel cats, but they're equally effective for blue cats. While small channel cats may peck at baits for several minutes before committing, big blues usually hit with the finesse of a freight train. Many veteran blue cat specialists place their rods in strong holders with the reel engaged and the drag locked tight. More often than not, a big blue cat will bury the hook point as it streaks off with the bait, doubling the rod over in the holder.

The best circle hook presentation for flatheads is the same one most anglers use with standard hook designs. After casting the bait, the rod is placed in a holder, in a boat or on shore, the clicker turned on, and the free-spool button engaged. When a flathead begins to move off—indicated by short bursts of the clicker— the rod is removed from the holder and the drive on the reel engaged. With the rod tip pointing at the fish, reel in slack line and lift steadily to drive the hook point into the corner of the fish's jaw. □

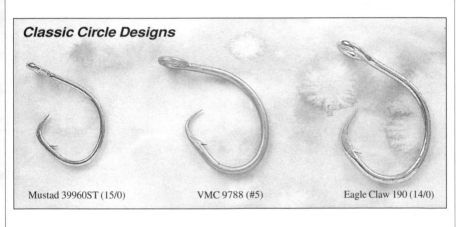

**Classic Circle Designs**

Mustad 39960ST (15/0)          VMC 9788 (#5)          Eagle Claw 190 (14/0)

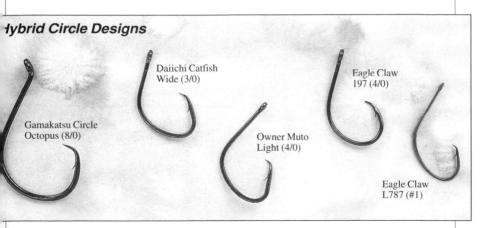

**Hybrid Circle Designs**

Gamakatsu Circle Octopus (8/0)

Daiichi Catfish Wide (3/0)

Owner Muto Light (4/0)

Eagle Claw 197 (4/0)

Eagle Claw L787 (#1)

# A MOBILE APPROACH FOR ICE PIKE

**B**ig pike are available to more anglers through the ice than during the open-water season. In most areas, pike aren't being targeted. In reservoirs in the Dakotas and across the Mountain West; in lakes in Iowa and Minnesota; in backwaters off the Mississippi River; and in many bays of the Great Lakes, panfish and walleyes are being fished for, but not so often pike. In areas where anglers do set up for pike, most of them plant a shack in a bay at first-ice and stay there for the rest of the season. This fishing demands mobility. Granted, tip-ups key fishing for pike. But tip-ups don't have to be a totally stationary presentation; that is, in most situations, they shouldn't be set in the same spot for more than a few hours.

## Quick-Strike Rigs

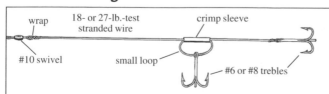

wrap   18- or 27-lb.-test stranded wire   crimp sleeve

#10 swivel   small loop

#6 or #8 trebles

## When

# Tackle

*Tip-ups:* stationary or wind tip-ups. *Line:* 36-pound-test dacron or teflon-coated ice line.

# Rigging

Use quick-strike rigs consisting of two #6 or #8 trebles rigged in tandem on 12- to 27-pound-test stranded wire. The distance between the hooks depends on the size of the bait. As good as deadbait can be for pike, livebait often attracts more fish. Use the liveliest 5- or 6-inch shiners or chubs you can find. Hook bait-fish so they swim down and away from the rigging—the end treble behind the head and the top treble near the dorsal fin.

# Location

Typical habitat areas in lakes include weededges in bays, particularly points and pockets in the edge; main-lake flats or bars with weedgrowth; and occasionally, rocky points, especially points that are part of a sunken island near classic shallow weedy habitat. In river backwaters, probe along weededges, the edges of the deepest holes in the backwater, and where current runs adjacent to the opening of the backwater. In reservoirs, try flats and channel cuts in the back end of creek arms; then work your way back out of the arm, checking each point along the way.

# Presentation

On a typical spot, set several tip-ups in various areas that pike prowl—along the deep edge of points or in pockets in a weededge, and in open pockets on the weed flat. On rocky areas, set tip-ups on the rock flat near the drop along the crest of the main drop-off, and at the base of the drop-off. In small areas, give pike an hour to respond. In larger areas, give them two hours. If pike don't bite within this time, or if the action stops, don't wait for a change in their aggressiveness. Move to another area. □

## Depth Zones For Tip-Ups

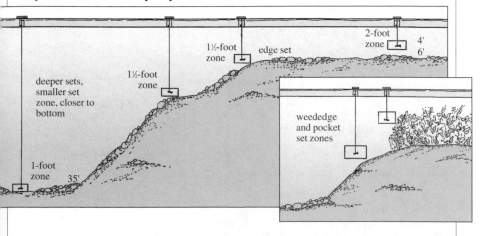

deeper sets, smaller set zone, closer to bottom

1½-foot zone

1-foot zone    35'

1½-foot zone

edge set

1½-foot zone

2-foot zone    4'    6'

weededge and pocket set zones

# SPOON SPECTRUMS FOR PIKE

Sometimes the difference between what you catch with one spoon and another is the difference between a dime and a dollar. This is due to differences in the flash, profile, and particularly the wobble of various spoons. For most fishermen, though, spoons are spoons, and they have, lying in their tackle box, one of these and two of those, and maybe four of those in five different colors and three different sizes. We suggest a more systematic approach to stocking up, assembling spectrums of spoon designs and sizes.

## When

## Tackle

*Rods:* A 7½-foot flippin' stick for 3/4- to 1½-ounce spoons and a 6½- to 7½-foot muskie bucktail rod for heavier models. Reels: medium- to large-capacity baitcasting reel. Line: 14-pound monofilament for lighter lures and 20-pound mono or 30-pound dacron for heavier baits.

# Rigging

*Size:* One standard spoon spectrum for Eppinger spoons looks like this: Huskie Devle (3¼ ounces, 5½ x 2½ inches), Huskie Junior (2 ounces, 4½ x 2 inches), Troll Devle (1¼ ounces, 3⅝ x 1¼ inches), Dardevle (1 ounce, 3⅝ x 1¼ inches), and Dardevlet (3/4 ounce, 2⅞ by 1⅜6 inch). These are classic pike spoons made of heavy stamped metal. The shapes change only slightly with each size change.

*Color:* Three top colors include the #17 Yellow with

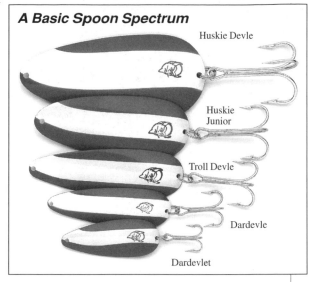

**A Basic Spoon Spectrum**

Huskie Devle
Huskie Junior
Troll Devle
Dardevle
Dardevlet

Red Diamonds (brass belly), #16 Red and White Stripe (nickel belly), and #58 Hot Mackerel (chartreuse and orange with brass belly). Maintain a spectrum of each color. Silver-bellied spoons shine in clear water, while brass-bellied colors are best in stained water. Stripes, scales, or hammering aren't visible when the spoons are moving. Try experimenting with colors that match the forage in the lake you're fishing.

*Vibration:* Vibration and sound patterns precede the fish's ability to see what's coming, even in the clearest water. Via vibration, they sense that something's there, something's coming before they see it. And pike are one of the most vibration-sensitive fish in freshwater. The heavy low-frequency thumping of a big spoon produces when the tinklings of smaller spoons attract only smaller fish. Those bigger pike often are conditioned to feeding on one- and two-pound walleyes and whitefish. □

**Top Color Patterns**

These three color patterns are top producers. The red-and-white with chrome belly, which has accounted for more pike than any other pattern, is particularly good in clearer water. The hot-chartreuse-and-orange with brass belly is good in dirtier or brown-stained water. The yellow five-of-diamonds with brass belly is good in brown-stained water so common in the North Country.

# SHORTLINE TROLLING FOR MUSKIES

**M**uskies can swim at speed bursts of approximately 17 miles per hour, which is far faster than any muskie lure can be reeled or trolled. So speeds of 7, even 8 mph, are not daunting to these fresh-water kingpins. In late summer, seemingly extreme speeds become a triggering factor. Historically, when pike and muskies seemed to turn off during the dog days of summer, fishermen contrived tales of tooth loss. It also was thought that the fish were slowing from the heat, when in fact the opposite was true. To trigger a response from these super-charged predators, more speed might be needed.

## Tackle

*Rods:* 8- to 10-foot heavy-power Dipsy rods with a slow action for planer boards and 6-foot heavy-power trolling rods for downrods. *Reels:* large-capacity saltwater-style baitcasting reels. *Line:* 50- to 80-pound braided line with 6-foot 80-pound monofilament leader.

## Rigging

The same basic rig is used to present high-speed crankbaits on planer boards and downlines. Begin by terminating the main line with a heavy coast-lock-type snap swivel. Next, tie another

**When**

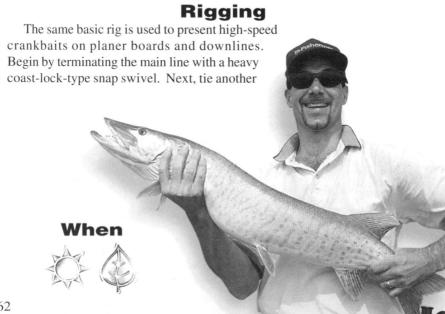

## Basic Setup Used On All Rods

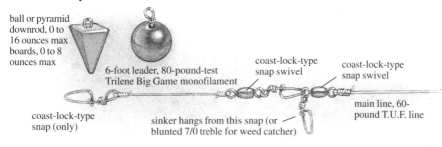

ball or pyramid downrod, 0 to 16 ounces max boards, 0 to 8 ounces max

6-foot leader, 80-pound-test Trilene Big Game monofilament

coast-lock-type snap swivel

coast-lock-type snap swivel

main line, 60-pound T.U.F. line

coast-lock-type snap (only)

sinker hangs from this snap (or blunted 7/0 treble for weed catcher)

snap swivel to one end of a 6-foot 80-pound-test mono leader and attach a coast-lock snap to the other end. Now hook the snap portion of the snap swivel on the leader to the swivel on the main line. A 2- to 16-ounce sinker can be attached to the hanging snap to allow the lure additional depth and to catch weeds and other debris.

## Location

Prime muskie flats in lakes are 15 to 35 feet deep, and they may or may not be adjacent to spawning bays. The real key is diversity. Muskies use diverse areas because, as tracking studies reveal, they sometimes set up in several home ranges throughout the year. Flats bordering extensive weedbeds and rocky shorelines and points are prime areas. Deep basins nearby can be key, especially in lakes with suspending forage fish. And diversity on the flats helps. Small humps and rises, rock-piles, beds of skunkweed or chara, and bottom transitions offer more habitat for a wider range of fish. And all fish are bait for muskies.

## Presentation

Short-line trolling produces open-water muskies throughout the season, but determining which part of the system is producing best on a given day is key to maximizing your catch rate. On bright calm days board lines might produce more fish, but downlines might be more productive on dark, overcast, or windy days. Try different lure styles, colors, and trolling speeds until you determine what works, then switch the rest of your trolling spread to the productive pattern. □

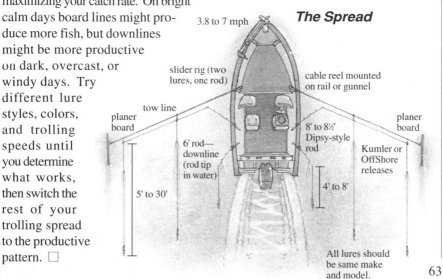

**The Spread**

3.8 to 7 mph

slider rig (two lures, one rod)

cable reel mounted on rail or gunnel

tow line

planer board

6' rod— downline (rod tip in water)

8' to 8½' Dipsy-style rod

planer board

Kumler or OffShore releases

5' to 30'

4' to 8'

All lures should be same make and model.

# TROLLING JERKBAITS FOR MUSKIES

Tracking studies indicate that muskies suspend more than most anglers think. They also move long distances across open water toward prime feeding locations. They may regularly move miles per day, spending short periods on shallow water structures, and then back across open water toward their next destination. If you're casting to shallow structure and not seeing fish, or fish are following your lure without striking, it may be time to give trolling a try.

## When

## Tackle

*Rod:* 6- to 7-foot heavy-action muskie jerkbait rod. *Reel:* large-capacity bait-casting reel. *Line:* 36-pound-test dacron.

## Location

During late summer and fall, muskies frequently roam between structural elements. Troll jerkbaits along a weededge; along or over rock bars or sand bars; along timber edges; over flats filled with fallen timber; and over sunken humps. In rivers, lakes, and reservoirs—almost anywhere muskies swim—trolled jerkbaits are an option.

## Presentation

For trolling, jerkbaits fall into two categories: those with a gliding side-to-side action and those with a diving up-and-down action. Gliding jerkbaits don't move consistently unless you stand up while trolling. To keep them working steadily from side to side, point your rod tip down and jerk the rod tip down about 6 inches. This sends the plug darting several feet left or right. Occasionally, it'll dive down or come to the surface. If you try to do this while sitting down, the bait will dart too erratically for even the most aggressive fish to hit.

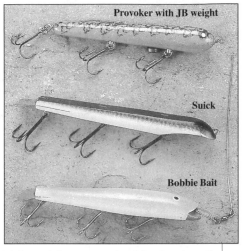

*Provoker with JB weight*

*Suick*

*Bobbie Bait*

With a diving jerkbait, sit down and hold the rod tip up or to the side. Don't troll too fast, but do keep your speed steady. Trolled slowly, a bait alternately dives a bit and floats up a bit, as the rod tip is jerked forward or up about a foot. Let the rod tip slowly drift back to its original position after each jerk. The forward movement of the boat keeps the line tight. A faster trolling speed makes the bait dive to a certain depth, but diminishes its up and down movement. The result is a jerk-forward, stop, jerk-forward, stop action. Increase lure depth by letting out more line, switching to lighter line, or using wire line. Also experiment with weighted jerkbaits, or weight standard baits by drilling holes and adding lead. ☐

## *Late Summer And Fall Locations*

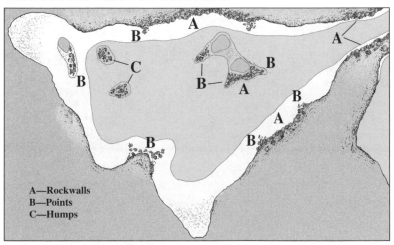

A—Rockwalls
B—Points
C—Humps

Many potential muskie locations in late summer and fall are associated with the main-lake basin. Trolling multiple structural elements dramatically increases your odds of contacting muskies.

# WIRE LEADERS FOR PIKE & MUSKIES

L osing jigs, crankbaits, and other lures intended for North Country bass to small razor-toothed pike is disappointing. Even worse to lose a big pike or muskie. Wire leaders help land toothy critters and other species like bass. And the right wire is so soft, supple, and thin that it's less visible than monofilament of the same breaking strength. Wire leaders may actually improve your catch.

## When

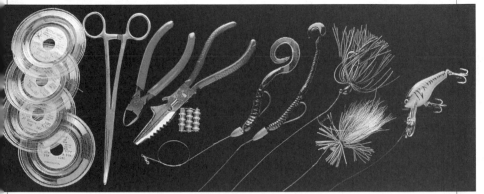

# Rigging

***Single Strand:*** Single-strand wire is relatively stiff, although wire testing under about 27 pounds remains rather supple because it's thin. It couples well with rubber-legged jigs, spinnerbaits, and crankbaits. But it isn't pliable enough for soft plastic worms and jerkbaits. Single-strand wire also is durable. Often, dozens of fish can be caught on the same leader. Although it may bend, if it doesn't kink and pull tight, use a wire straightener tool to remove the bends and keep fishing.

Construct single-strand leaders by slipping one end of the wire through the eye of a hook, snap, or swivel, leaving about a 3-inch tag end. With your fingers, make 5 loose wraps (about an inch), then bend the tag end perpendicular to the main wire. Grip the top of the wraps with a pliers and make 10 more tight wraps (about 1/4-inch) with your fingers. Trim the tag end close to the wraps and repeat.

***Stranded Wire:*** Stranded wire is made from fine wire strands wrapped together to make a softer, more supple wire than single-strand. Stranded wire often is called "braided" wire, but that's a misnomer since the fibers aren't braided. Most stranded wires consist of either 3 or 7 wire strands. Three-stranded wire comes in 8- or 12-pound break strengths, which is fine bite-off protection for bass and walleye rigs. Seven-strand wire comes in break strengths of 18 to over 100 pounds for pike and muskie leaders.

To construct a leader with stranded wire, slip the end of the wire twice through the eye of a hook, snap, or swivel, leaving about a 2-inch tag end. Next, clip a forceps to the tag end. Hold the hook with one hand and the main wire with the other—leave the forceps dangling. Now swing the forceps around the main wire, wrapping progressively forward for about an inch. Trim the tag close to the main wire and repeat the process on the other end of the leader. □

# GLOSSARY

*Action:* Measure of rod performance that describes the bend of a rod; ranges from slow to fast.

*Anal Fin:* Fin located on the ventral side of most fish, between the anal pore and tail.

*Backwater:* Shallow area off a river.

*Baitfish:* Small fish often eaten by predators.

*Bar:* Long ridge in a body of water. Sometimes called a shoal.

*Bay:* Major indentation in the shoreline of a lake or reservoir.

*Bell Sinker:* Pear-shaped sinker with brass eye on top.

*Break:* Distinct variation in otherwise constant stretch of cover, structure, or bottom type.

*Breakline:* Area of abrupt change in depth, bottom type, or water quality.

*Cabbage:* Any of several species of submerged weeds of the genus Potamogeton.

*Canal:* Manmade waterway for navigation.

*Channel:* The bed of a stream or river.

*Coontail:* Submerged aquatic plant of the hornwort family, typically found in hard water; characterized by stiff, forked leaves.

*Cove:* An indentation along the shoreline of a lake or reservoir.

*Cover:* Natural or manmade objects on the bottom of lakes, rivers, or impoundments, especially those that influence fish behavior.

*Crankbait:* Lipped diving lure.

*Crustacean:* Hard-shelled, typically aquatic invertebrate.

*Current:* Water moving in one direction, which may be interrupted or redirected over objects.

*Dam:* Manmade barrier to water flow.

*Dark-Bottom Bay:* Shallow, protected bay with a layer of dark organic material on the bottom that warms quickly in spring.

*Dorsal Fin:* Fin located on center of a fish's back.

*Drag:* System for allowing fish to pull line from reel while antireverse switch is engaged.

*Drainage:* The area drained by a river and its tributaries.

*Drop-Off:* An area of substantial increase in depth.

*Eddy:* Area of slack water or reversed current in a stream or river.

*Egg Sinker:* Egg-shaped sinker with a hole from end to end.

*Farm Pond:* Small manmade body of water.

*Feeder Creek:* Tributary to a stream.

*Feeding Strategy:* Behaviors used for capturing prey.

*Fingerling:* Juvenile fish, usually from 1 to 3 inches long.

*Fishing Pressure:* Amount of angling on a body of water in a period of time, usually measured in hours per acre per year; its effects on fish populations.

**Flat:** Area of lake, reservoir, or river characterized by little change in depth; may be shallow or deep.

**Flippin':** Presentation technique for dropping lures into dense cover at close range.

**Flippin' Stick:** Heavy-action fishing rod, 7 to 8 feet long, originally designed for bass fishing.

**Float:** Buoyant device for suspending bait.

**Float Stop:** Adjustable rubber bead or thread placed on line above float to determine fishing depth.

**Fluorescent:** Emits radiation when exposed to sunlight.

**Forage:** Something to be eaten; the act of eating.

**Front:** Weather system that causes changes in temperature, cloud cover, precipitation, wind, and barometric pressure.

**Fry:** Recently hatched fish.

**Gamefish:** Fish species pursued by anglers.

**Habitat:** Type of environment in which an organism usually lives.

**Hole:** Deep section of a stream or river.

**Hybrid:** Offspring of two species or subspecies.

**Impoundment:** Body of water formed by damming running water (a reservoir).

**Invertebrate:** Animal without a backbone.

**Jig:** Lure composed of leadhead with rigid hook, often with hair, plastic, rubber, or other dressings.

**Lake:** Confined area where water accumulates naturally.

**Larva:** Immature form of an organism.

**Lateral Line:** Sensory system of fish that detects low frequency vibrations in water.

**Ledge:** Sharp contour break in a river or reservoir.

**Livebait:** Any living animal used to entice fish to bite.

**Location:** Where fish position themselves in a body of water.

**Migration:** Directed movement by large number of animals of one species.

**Minnowbait:** Long, thin, minnow-shaped wood or plastic lure; a wobbling bait.

**Monofilament:** Fishing line made from a strand of synthetic fiber.

**Nymph:** Larval form of an insect.

**Omnivore:** Organism that eats a wide variety of items.

**Open Water:** The portion of a lake or reservoir away from flats and shoals.

**Opportunistic:** Feeding strategy in which items are eaten according to availability.

**Overharvest:** A level of fish harvest from a body of water that substantially reduces abundance of catchable fish, particularly large fish.

**Oxbow:** A U-shaped bend in a river.

**Panfish:** Group of about 30 small warmwater sportfish, including bullheads but not catfish.

**Pattern:** A defined set of location and presentation factors that consistently produce fish.

**Pectoral Fin:** Paired fin usually located on fish's side behind the head.

**Pelagic:** Living in open, offshore waters.

**Pelvic Fin:** Paired fin usually located on lower body.

**pH:** A measure of acidity or alkalinity.

**Phosphorescent:** Ability to glow in the dark after exposure to a light source.

**Pit:** Area excavated for mining operations that fills with water.

**Pitching:** Presentation technique in which worms or jigs are dropped into cover at close range (15 to 30 feet) with an underhand, pendulum motion, using a 6- to 7-foot casting rod.

**Plankton:** Organisms drifting in a body of water.

**Plug:** Solid-bodied wood or plastic lure.

**Point:** Projection of land into a body of water.

**Polarized:** Capability of breaking up sunlight into directional components.

**Pond:** Small natural or manmade body of water.

**Pool:** Deep section of a stream or river.

**Population:** Group of animals of the same species within a geographical area that freely interbreed.

**Postspawn:** Period immediately after spawning; In-Fisherman calendar period between spawn and presummer.

**Pound-Test:** System for measuring the strength of fishing line; the amount of pressure that will break a line.

**Predator:** A fish that often feeds on other fish.

**Presentation:** Combination of bait or lure, rig, tackle, and technique used to catch fish.

**Prespawn:** Period prior to spawning; In-Fisherman calendar period between winter and spawn.

**Prey:** Fish that often are eaten by other fish species.

**Prop Bait:** Topwater plug with one or more propellers at the front or back.

**Range:** Area over which a species is distributed.

**Rattlebait:** Hollow-bodied, sinking, lipless crankbaits that rattle loudly due to shot and slugs in the body cavity.

**Reeds:** Any of several species of tall, leafless emergent aquatic weeds that grow in shallow zones of lakes and reservoirs.

**Reef:** Rocky hump in a body of water.

**Reservoir:** Large manmade body of water.

**Resting Spot:** Location used by fish not actively feeding.

**Riffle:** Shallow, fast flowing section of a stream or river.

**Rig:** Arrangement of components for bait-fishing, including hooks, leader, sinker, swivel, beads.

**Riprap:** Large rocks placed along a bank to prevent erosion.

**Riverine:** Having characteristics of a river.

**Run:** Straight, moderate-depth section of a stream or river with little depth change.

**School:** Group of fish of one species moving in unison.

**Selective Harvest:** Releasing or harvesting fish, based on species, size, and relative abundance.

**Sensory Organ:** Biological system involved in sight, hearing, taste, smell, touch, or lateral line sense.

**Set Rig:** Rig cast into position on the bottom to await a strike.

**Shot:** Small round sinkers pinched onto fishing line.

**Silt:** Fine sediment on the bottom of a body of water.

**Sinkers:** Variously shaped pieces of lead used to sink a bait or lure.

**Slipfloat:** Float with hole for sliding freely on line.

**Slipsinker:** Sinker with a hole for sliding freely on line.

**Slop:** Dense aquatic vegetation matted on the surface.

**Slough:** Cove or backwater of a reservoir or river.

**Slow Roll:** Spinnerbait presentation in which the lure is retrieved slowly through and over cover objects.

**Snag:** Brush or tree in a stream or river.

**Solitary:** Occupying habitat without close association to others.

**Sonar:** Electronic fishing aid that emits sound waves underwater and interprets them to depict underwater objects.

**Spawn:** Reproduction of fish; In-Fisherman calendar period associated with that activity.

**Species:** Group of potentially interbreeding organisms.

**Spine:** Stiff, sharp segment of fin.

**Spoon:** Any of a variety of metal, plastic, or wood lures with a generally spoonlike shape and a single hook.

**Sportfish:** Fish species pursued by anglers.

**Stock:** Plant fish in a body of water.

**Stress:** State of physiological imbalance caused by disturbing environmental factors.

**Strike:** Biting motion of a fish.

**Strike Window (Zone):** Conceptual area in front of a fish within which it will strike food items or lures.

**Structure:** Changes in the shape of the bottom of lakes, rivers, or impoundments, especially those that influence fish behavior.

**Stumpfield:** Area of an impoundment where stands of timber have been cut prior to impoundment, leaving stumps below the surface.

**Substrate:** Type of bottom in a body of water.

**Suspended Fish:** Fish in open water hovering considerably above bottom.

**Swim (Gas) Bladder:** Organ of most bony fish that holds a volume of gas to make them neutrally buoyant at variable depths.

**Tailwater:** Area immediately downstream from a dam.

**Temperature Tolerant:** Able to function in a range of temperatures.

**Terminal Tackle:** Components of a baitfishing system including hooks, sinkers, swivels, and leaders.

**Thermocline:** Layer of water with abrupt change in temperature, occurring between warm surface layer and cold bottom layer.

**Topwaters:** Lures designed to be worked on the surface.

**Tracking:** Following radio-tagged or sonic-tagged animals.

**Trailer:** A plastic skirt, grub, pork rind, livebait, or other attractor attached to a lure to entice fish.

**Trailer Hook:** An extra hook attached to a lure's rear hook to catch fish that strike behind the lure.

**Transducer:** Electronic part of a sonar unit that receives sound impulses and converts them to visual images.

**Tributary:** Stream or river flowing into a larger river.

**Trigger:** Characteristics of a lure or bait presentation that elicit a biting response in fish.

**Trolling:** Fishing method in which lures or baits are pulled by a boat.

**Trolling Motor:** Electric motor positioned on the bow or transom to push or pull the boat.

**Turbid:** Murky water, discolored by suspended sediment.

**Turbulence:** Water disturbed by strong currents.

**Waterdog:** Immature salamander possessing external gills.

**Watershed:** The region draining runoff into a body of water.

**Weed:** Aquatic plant.

**Weedline (Weededge):** Abrupt edge of a weedbed caused by a change in depth, bottom type, or other factor.

**Wing Dam:** Manmade earth or rock ridge designed to deflect current.

**Winterkill:** Fish mortality due to oxygen depletion under the ice.

# GOOD FISHING TO YOU FROM YOUR FRIENDS AT IN-FISHERMAN!

The In-Fisherman Secrets Series presents inside information on a range of fishing topics.

For more information about freshwater fishing, In-Fisherman also offers books and videos that detail fishing tactics for largemouth bass, smallmouth bass, walleye, northern pike, muskie, catfish, crappies and other panfish, plus trout. Ice fishing's covered too. And many more select topics.

We're just a bunch of crazy fishheads who love it all and want to help you catch more fish and have more fun. For more information, call 218/829-1648, or visit our Web site <www.in-fisherman.com>.